Perspectives in American Education

THE MELTING
OF
THE ETHNICS:
Education of the
Immigrants, 1880-1914
By
Mark Krug

PHI DELTA KAPPA
Educational Foundation
Bloomington, Indiana

Perspectives in American Education

This book is one of a five-volume set published by Phi Delta Kappa as part of its national bicentennial year program.
The other titles in the set are:

The Purposes of Education, by Stephen K. Bailey
Values in Education, by Max Lerner
Alternatives in Education, by Vernon Smith, Robert Barr, and Daniel Burke
Women in Education, by Patricia C. Sexton

Introduction

The two hundredth anniversary of the American declaration of separation from the government of England has stimulated millions of words of sentiment, analysis, nostalgia, and expectation. Much of this verbal and pictorial outpouring has been a kind of patriotic breast-beating. Most of it has been rhetoric.

Several years ago the leadership of Phi Delta Kappa announced its determination to offer a significant contribution to the bicentennial celebration in a series of authoritative statements about major facets of American education that would deserve the attention of serious scholars in education, serve the needs of neophytes in the profession, and survive as an important permanent contribution to the educational literature.

The Board of Directors and staff of Phi Delta Kappa, the Board of Governors of the Phi Delta Kappa Educational Foundation, and the Project '76 Implementation Committee all made important contributions to the creation of the Bicentennial Activities Program, of which this set of books is only one of seven notable projects. The entire program has been made possible by the loyal contributions of dedicated Kappans who volunteered as Minutemen, Patriots, and Bell Ringers according to the size of their donations and by the support of the Educational Foundation, based on the generous bequest of George Reavis. The purpose of the Foundation, as stated at its inception, is to contribute to a better understanding of the educative process and the relation of education to human welfare. These five volumes should serve that purpose well.

A number of persons should be recognized for their contributions to the success of this enterprise. The Board of Governors of the Foundation, under the leadership of Gordon Swanson, persevered in the early planning stages to insure that the effort would be made. Other members of the board during this period were Edgar Dale, Bessie Gabbard, Arliss Roaden, Howard Soule, Bill Turney, and Ted Gordon, now deceased.

The Project '76 Implementation Committee, which wrestled successfully with the myriad details of planning, financing, and publicizing the seven activities, included David Clark, Jack Frymier, James Walden, Forbis Jordan, and Ted Gordon.

The Board of Directors of Phi Delta Kappa, 1976 to 1978, include President Bill L. Turney, President-Elect Gerald Leischuck, Vice-Presidents William K. Poston, Rex K. Reckewey, and Ray Tobiason and District Representatives Gerald L. Berry, Jerome G. Kopp, James York, Cecil K. Phillips, Don Park, Philip G. Meissner, and Carrel Anderson.

The major contributors to this set of five perspectives on American education are of course the authors. They have found time in busy professional schedules to produce substantial and memorable manuscripts, both scholarly and readable. They have things to say about education that are worth saying, and they have said them well. They have made a genuine contribution to the literature, helping to make a fitting contribution to the celebration of two hundred years of national freedom. More importantly, they have articulated ideas so basic to the maintenance of that freedom that they should be read and heeded as valued guidelines for the years ahead, hopefully at least another two hundred.

—Lowell Rose
Executive Secretary
Phi Delta Kappa

Contents

1

Multicultural Education

Sociologists writing in the 1940s and '50s about future trends in American society were sure that America
was rapidly becoming a homogeneous society. They predicted that in a few decades, the separate white ethnic
groups would disappear by total assimilation in the dominant society. In 1945 W. Lloyd Warner and Leo Srole
wrote in *The Social Systems of American Ethnic Groups:*
> The. future of American ethnic groups seems to be
> limited; it is likely that they will be quickly absorbed.
> Paradoxically, the force of American equalitarianism,
> which attempts to make all men American and alike, and
> the force of our class order, which creates differences
> among ethnic peoples, have combined to dissolve our
> ethnic groups.

Talcott Parsons predicted the gradual disappearance of
the white ethnic groups. These minorities, he maintained,
could not long endure as separate entities in a central-
ized and primary group; they must soon give way to the
emerging technologically advanced society. Louis Wirth
concluded that the ghettos created by the Jewish immigrants represented their desire to transplant the

European "shtetlech" (little towns in Russia and Poland) on the American soil. While he saw some admirable features in the life of the ghetto, he was certain that the second and third generations of American Jews would move out of their neighborhoods and forsake their ethnic loyalties and identity.

The New Ethnics

It is evident, as we enter the last quarter of the century, that these predictions have proven to be false. Where did these eminent sociologists go wrong? They did not and could not foresee the great changes that were to take place in the decade or two after their studies were completed. If the trends in American society had continued as they were when Warner, Srole, Parsons, and Wirth made their studies, the separate white ethnic groups may indeed have gradually disappeared. But major unforeseen events have occurred, as usual, and the fallout from these unexpected developments has given a new life and vitality to the major white ethnic groups in America.

First in importance and in impact is the civil rights revolution in the black community. The partially successful struggle of the blacks for equal political and economic rights, bolstered by civil rights laws enacted by Congress and by large expenditures of federal money to improve the education and the economic standards of Negroes, had a great impact on the major white ethnic groups. This was particularly true of the largely blue-collar Poles, Hungarians, Italians, Serbs, and Slovaks and the rapidly growing community of the Spanish-speaking immigrants. These groups responded to the demands for black studies, and to the slogans of "Black Power" and "Black is Beautiful," with demands for more attention to their needs and aspirations, and for a greater appreciation of their values and contributions. Poles in Chicago and Milwaukee, Italians in Newark and New Haven took to wearing buttons proclaiming "Polish is Beautiful" and "Italian Power." Simultaneously, the cohesion and loyalty of the Jews in America were greatly strengthened by two traumatic events in their history, the killing by the Nazis of 6 million Jews and the creation of the state of Israel.

The growing political and economic instability and the rapid discarding of many established social values and mores have contributed to the search by the second and third generations of descendants of immigrants for their ethnic roots and values. Many of them apparently found comfort, a sense of belonging, and greater security in participating in weddings, dances, and cultural or political events sponsored by their respective ethnic groups. The old and stable customs and ways of their respective minority groups seem to provide the needed anchor in their lives.

Msgr. Geno Baroni, a leader of Italian-Americans and President of the National Center for Urban Ethnic Studies, asserts that public policy, as pursued by Congress and the federal government, neglects white ethnic groups in programs aimed at saving the inner cities from decay and destruction. In his view, the federal government ignores the substandard housing and poor schools of Poles, Italians, Serbs, and Slovaks, who, because of their low economic status, have no choice but stay in their enclaves in the inner cities. Baroni wrote that because American social problems were defined in the context of poverty and vice, it was impossible to deal with social issues in terms of distributing resources, rights, and privileges among different groups. Andrew Greeley of the National Center for Opinion Research, who writes extensively on ethnicity and the white ethnics observed,

> Since it is assumed that most ethnic groups ought to vanish (except for Jews, blacks, Spanish-speaking Americans and American Indians) and since it is also assumed that most ethnic groups have no contribution to make, it is scarcely worth learning anything about them. Italians provide pizza, Poles provide Polish jokes, and Irish pro-

vide corrupt politicians. . . . Well they're all going to go
away too.

Greeley assails the forced assimilation of the immigrants
and pokes fun at the melting pot "myth." He argues that
most blacks look upon revived ethnic awareness as a
white backlash because they fail to realize that the new
ethnic awareness is due to the legitimization of cultural
pluralism by the blacks.

Barbara Mikulski, a member of the Baltimore City
Council, pleads for the preservation of the ethnic neighborhoods with their churches, clubs, and taverns, and
their special sets of values. She argues that ethnic pride
and consciousness could provide a richness that America
now lacks.

Baroni, Greeley, and Mikulski make a convincing case
about the revival of ethnicity and ethnic awareness, but
their discussion of a rationale for a degree of separateness of the white ethnic groups is made difficult by their
confusion in the use of the concepts of "melting pot,"
"assimilation," and "cultural pluralism." It is important
to trace the historical origins of these concepts because
the indiscriminate and often erroneous use of these key
terms has obscured the important issue of the possible
effect of revived ethnic feelings and loyalties on the future structure of the American society. For instance, integration in housing patterns is not conducive to the survival
of ethnic values. Ethnicity as expressed in belonging to the
same clubs, organizations, churches, in separate religious
and language schools, and in restaurants demands a certain degree of segregation. For the Amish in Pennsylvania
and the Cajuns in Louisiana, the degree of self-segre-
gation is great indeed. Ethnic-minded Jews, Poles,
Greeks, Italians, and Lithuanians, when they move from
their old inner-city neighborhoods usually find other enclaves in other parts of the city or in the suburbs. Inte-
grated neighborhoods, are—the truth must be stated—
inimical to the survival of ethnic loyalties. This fact
raises the question of how to reconcile the legitimate
aspirations of the ethnic groups to live their lives as they

want to live them and to avoid further polarization in our already deeply divided and alienated society. Some see the solution in a "new pluralism." Before we try to understand this concept, let's take a closer look at the "old" pluralism and other related concepts.

The Concept of the Melting Pot

In *Beyond the Melting Pot*, published in 1957, Daniel P. Moynihan and Nathan Glazer concluded after studying several major ethnic groups in New York that the melting pot theory was not a total success because ethnic loyalties were experiencing a revival. That thesis has since been supported by other authors. Andrew Greeley in his *Why Can't They Be Like Us?*, Peter Schrag in *The Decline of the WASP*, Michael Novak in *The Rise of the Unmeltable Ethnics*, while differing on some issues, all agree that the conception of the United States as a homogeneous society in which the separate immigrant cultures have melted and have become absorbed into a predominant culture is false.

Michael Novak has denounced the melting pot theory, which, in his view, forced the children and grandchildren of various immigrant groups to renounce their ethnic mores and values. Novak wrote that "growing up in America has been an assault upon my sense of worthiness." In order to "make it" in the American society, he had to deny his Slovak heritage and even to loosen his ties to his family.

In hearings conducted by a House Subcommittee on Education considering the Ethnic Heritage Studies Bill, which became law in 1973, several spokesmen for white ethnic groups repeatedly declared in their testimony that the "melting pot" concept was dead, and the entire melting pot theory was a myth. They blamed the melting pot idea for driving the second and third generations of immigrants to assimilation into the homogenized mainstream American culture and to the desertion of their ethnic roots and heritage. Dr. Leonard Fein of Brandeis University testified that in spite of all the pressure for a "'melted society,' America remains a collection of groups, and not individuals, no matter how much liberals might wish it otherwise."

As we have said, some leaders of American Poles, Italians, Slovaks, Serbs, and others often use the term "Americanization" interchangeably with the concept of the melting pot. They equate the melting pot theory with the pressure exerted on the immigrants and their children and grandchildren to conform to the dominant Anglo-Saxon American culture. "Americanization for the immigrants from Southern and Eastern Europe," wrote Michael Novak, meant that they were "catechized, cajoled and condescended to by guardians of good Anglo-Saxon attitudes. . . ." Former Congressman Roman Pucinski defined the problem in his testimony before the committee: "This country has to recognize that we are individual human beings and this effort of trying to homogenize us into a solid single mold, be it puritan, atheist, or Anglo-Saxon, or what have you, is a myth and if the country is falling apart at the seams today, it is only because we have tried to deny ethnicity." Pucinski seems to blame the "myth" of the melting pot for all the ills that beset our society. The Rev. Jesse Jackson, an influential black leader, has also denounced the melting pot theory. "The whole notion of a melting pot," he states, "is perverted imagery. It has antagonized white people and black people because the melting pot is the integration concept . . . that everybody will become one race, a new race made up of the different people in the world." The originators of the melting pot concept, of course, never intended it to include the blacks in America. They were quite aware of the importance of the color factor. The theory envisaged the possible fusion of the "old" established American society and the waves of white immigrants who came to the United States at the turn of the twentieth century. Because of the difference in skin color, it did not and does not make much sense to talk about the melting pot theory in relation to black children.

Spokesmen for Anglo-Saxon or Nordic superiority who wrote at the turn of the century had little difficulty in distinguishing between the melting pot and Americanization theories as they applied to the immigrants. Leading American educators did not want the immigrants' children to fuse with the children of older American, Anglo-Saxon families. They wanted the immigrants and their children to accept the Anglo-Saxon values and ways of life and to forget their respective cultures.

A distinguished historian of American education and an educational leader of great influence, Elwood P. Cubberley advocated an intensive effort to Americanize the children of the immigrants. He clearly understood the difference between Americanization and the melting pot. The former he advocated, and the latter he rejected.

In his book, *Changing Conceptions of Education*, Cubberley wrote:

> About 1882, the character of our immigration from the north of Europe dropped off rather abruptly and in its place immigration from the south and east of Europe, set in and soon developed into a great stream. After 1880, southern Italians and Sicilians; people from all parts of that medley of races known as the Austro-Hungarian Empire: Czechs, Moravians, Slovaks, Poles, Jews, Ruthenians, Croatians, Servians (sic), Dalmatians, Slovenians, Magyars, Roumanians, Austrians . . . began to come in great numbers.
>
> The southern and eastern Europeans are a very different type from the north Europeans who preceded them. Illiterate, docile, lacking in self-reliance and initiative and possessing none of the Anglo-Teutonic conceptions of law, order and government, their coming has served to dilute tremendously our national stock, and to corrupt our civic life. . . .
>
> Our task is to break up their groups or settlements, to assimilate and to amalgamate these people as part of our American race, and to implant in their children, so far as can be done, the Anglo-Saxon conceptions of righteousness, law and order and popular government, and to awaken in them reverence for our democratic in-

stitutions and for those things in our national life which
we as people hold to be of abiding worth.

Reviews praised Cubberley's work, and few, if any,
challenged his xenophobic references to immigrants from
southern and eastern Europe or his notions about the
docility and the lack of initiative of the millions of Italians, Poles, Greeks, and Jews who in fact adjusted themselves to the American environment with relative ease.
Cubberley was not asked to clarify his use of the terms
"our national stock" or "American race," or to prove his
assumption about the devotion of the Nordics to the
"Anglo-Saxon conception of righteousness, law and
order." Even if the Hills, the Harrimans, the Rockefel-
lers, and the Morgans were not "robber barons," their
careers were not marked by unwavering support of
Anglo-Saxon virtues.

Cubberley felt that the obligation of the public schools
in areas of great immigrant concentrations was to assimilate the children of the newcomers into the superior
"American race." His view was generally accepted by
school administrators and teachers. On the whole, they
shared Cubberley's contempt for the cultures, values, and
mores of the immigrants. Clearly, these influential
Americans who dealt directly with the immigrants and
their children did not believe in the melting pot concept.
They favored Americanizing or Anglo-Saxonizing of the
immigrants.

One of the most outspoken advocates of Americanization
and an opponent of the influence of ethnic factors on American politics was Theodore Roosevelt. In a speech given in
1910, which he entitled "Americanism," Roosevelt said:

> There is no room in the country for hyphenated Ameri-
> canism. Our allegiance must be purely to the United
> States. For an American citizen to vote as a German-
> American, an Irish-American, or an Italian-American is to
> be a traitor to American institutions and those hyphenated
> Americans who terrorize politicians by threats of the
> foreign vote are engaged in treason to the American re-
> public.

Ethnic groups, Poles, Jews, Greeks, blacks, Chicanos have paid no heed to Roosevelt's injunctions. They consider it to be within their rights as American citizens to support the ethnic causes which they espouse. As a rule, they are convinced that their particular objectives in foreign policy which they pursue are consistent with the best interests of the United States.

Of course, most immigrants, even those who were determined to preserve their ethnic identity and who cherished their group values, did find it desirable or necessary to adjust to the American society and to the American way of life.

In an essay in *Ethnic Group Politics* (edited by Barley and Katz), Oscar Handlin described "A subtle process of adjustment [that] found each immigrant group drifting away from the particularities of its heritage and reaching out toward a more general view of itself that would confirm and strengthen its place in the whole society." There is ample evidence to indicate that in nearly all of the ethnic immigrant groups many individuals *wanted* to become Americanized fully or in part as soon as possible. They wanted their children to speak English, to play baseball, and to develop a taste for hamburgers. The traditional large-scale Fourth of July celebrations had no more enthusiastic participants than many thousands of newly arrived Jews, Irish, Italians, Poles, and others.

Jane Addams, the founder and director of Hull House in Chicago, had a more sophisticated and more perceptive insight as to the place and the needs of the immigrants, both adults and children, with whom she worked. She had a better appreciation of the actual working of the melting pot theory than did Cubberley and the school superintendents of large city school systems. While her friend and associate John Dewey showed little interest in the education of immigrant children, Jane Addams devoted a great deal of her time to the study of the problem. Miss Addams, living and working in the midst of the immigrant ghettos, developed a respect for her clients and for their respective cultures. She tells in her autobiography that loving and admiring Abraham Lincoln, as she did from her youth, she would always tell the immigrant children to be proud of their past and of their cultural heritage as Lincoln was proud of his youth in Kentucky, Indiana, and on the Illinois prairies. She deplored the forced isolation and alienation of the immigrants. In her view, their withdrawal into their enclaves was their response to the ridicule and contempt that they suffered from influential elements of the dominant society. She deplored the fact that intense dislike of the immigrants made the children and grandchildren of the newcomers ashamed of their heritage, their parents, their culture, and their customs.

The residents and the staff at Hull House were obligated to do chores for the families of the immigrants, to help the sick and the infirm, to take care of the small children while mothers were away, and even to prepare bodies for burial. Jane Addams saw this service as beneficial to her staff because it gave them an opportunity to get to know and to appreciate the life and the culture of the immigrants. Americanization to Jane Addams did not mean Anglo-Saxonizing the immigrants. To be sure she hoped to acculturate the immigrants and their children to the American society and its mainstream culture but she was convinced that America as a nation was still in a process of dynamic change and that the immigrants had much to contribute to the emergent and forming American culture. It is in this sense that Jane Addams used and understood the "melting pot" concept long before it became a widely used term.

The idea of America as a melting pot was first used by John de Crevecoeur who wrote in 1756, "Here in America individuals of all nations are melted into a new race of men." That concept was elaborated upon by Israel Zangwill, a British writer who in 1908 wrote a play entitled *The Melting Pot*. The play was produced on Broadway and met with great success. In the play, the hero, a young Jewish violinist, an immigrant from Russia, speaks these lines:

America is God's Crucible, the great Melting Pot where all the races of Europe are melting and reforming! Here you stand good folk, think I, when I see you at Ellis Island, here you stand, in your fifty groups, with your fifty languages and histories, and your fifty blood hatreds and rivalries. But you won't be long like that, brothers, for these are the fires of God you come to—these are the fires of God. A fig for your feuds and vendettas! German and Frenchmen, Irishmen and English, Jews and Russians, into the Crucible with you all! God is making the American.

There is little common ground between Zangwill's melting pot theory and Cubberley's theory of Americanization, his assumption of the existence of an American race, his belief in Anglo-Saxon superiority, or his advocacy of the use of schools to Americanize the children of the immigrants. While Cubberley looked with contempt on the cultural heritage of the immigrants and demanded their assimilation into the Anglo-Saxon dominant culture, Zangwill welcomed the contributions of Italians, Poles, Jews, Russians, Slovaks, and others. The melting pot theory assumed that American culture was like a mighty river that gratefully receives the variety of flows from the many tributary rivers representing the various cultures of the immigrant groups. According to Zangwill, the constant input of the tributaries changes and enriches the great river. The immigrants are not forced to become Americans by desertion of their cultures, but by the melting or adjusting of their cultural heritages to the dominant culture. This process would eventually produce a unique, superior race and a superior culture. "The real American," Zangwill wrote, "has not yet arrived. He is only in the Crucible. I tell you— he will be the *fusion* of *all races*, perhaps the coming superman."

The advocates of the melting pot theory deplored the hatreds and feuds that the immigrants brought with them from Europe and perpetuated in America, but they acknowledged that there was much good in their respective cultures. They believed that the new, emerging American culture must be built not on the destruction of the cultural values and mores of the various immigrant groups but on their *fusion* with the existing American civilization, which itself was never purely Anglo-Saxon but a product of the interaction of Anglo-Saxon elements with the French, the Irish, the Dutch, the American Indians, and the blacks.

The melting pot concept presupposes respect for the cultural heritage of the immigrants because it accepts their intrinsic values and their potential contribution to the cultural melting process, which was and is taking place on American soil. This process envisaged the emergence of a new American people from the crucible of American pluralistic society.

Finally, the melting pot theorists rejected the notion, expressed by Cubberley and other nativist spokesmen, of the superiority of the Nordic, Anglo-Saxon race. In the burning fires of the melting pot, all races were equal—all were reshaped, and molded into a new entity. Readiness to sacrifice part of one's ethnic culture for the common good was required, but in the process of creating a new nation, all cultures and all cultural strains were important factors.

The "Americanization" Idea

The confusion between the terms "Americanization" and the melting pot has recently become so widespread that it makes an intelligent discussion of ethnicity, of ethnic education or "multi-cultural" education difficult, if not impossible. Those who proclaim that the melting pot idea was a myth or that it is dead obviously confuse that idea with the theory of Americanization. They are obviously unaware that Zangwill's term, which was consequently refined and elaborated upon by sociologists into a social theory, aroused strong opposition among the advocates of outright Americanization of the immigrants.

In 1926, Henry Pratt Fairchild, one of the most distinguished American sociologists of his time, published a book entitled *The Melting Pot Mistake*, which met with great critical acclaim. Fairchild argued that while the racial makeup of the American people would be hard to define, an American nationality did exist, based on Nordic or Anglo-Saxon cultural values and mores. The American nation, according to Fairchild, was formed principally by immigrants from England, Ireland, Germany, and the Scandinavian countries. But "beginning about 1882," he wrote, "the immigration problem in the United States has become increasingly a racial problem in two distinct ways, first by altering profoundly the Nordic predominance in the American population, and second by introducing various new elements which are so different from any of the old ingredients that even small quantities are deeply significant." These "new elements" consisted of Italians, Poles, and Jews, who were coming to the United States in large numbers. "The American people," Fairchild argued, "have since the revolution resisted any threat of dilution by a widely different race and must continue to do so in the case of large-scale immigration. If they fail to do so, the American nation would face the beginning of the process of mongrelization."

The "melting pot" idea, according to Fairchild, was "slowly, insidiously, irresistably eating away the very heart of the United States. What was being melted in the great Melting Pot, losing all form and symmetry, all beauty and character, all nobility and usefulness, was the American nationality itself."

What the immigrants had to be told, with great kindness and full consideration, according to Fairchild, was that they were welcome to the United States *under the condition* that they would renounce their respective cultural values and embrace the dominant culture forged by the predominantly Nordic American people since its independence. The American public schools must be made the effective tools of achieving this objective, at least as far as the children of the immigrants were concerned. And this process must be accomplished as fast as possible.

Obviously, the melting pot concept and theory had a different meaning for Fairchild than it has for those who write on behalf of the white ethnic groups today.

However, for many immigrants in the '20s and '30s,

or at least for those who wished to maintain their ethnic identity, neither the Americanization concept, nor the melting pot theory were acceptable. That was particularly true of some Jews, Poles, Italians, Slovaks, Greeks, Serbs, Croatians, and others. For many of them, Americanization meant forceful assimilation, the acceptance of a cultural gap, and often a rift between the older and the younger generation. The melting pot theory, while predicated on an attitude of respect for ethnic cultures, also envisioned as the end result of the process an emergence of a new, fused American culture. That fact presented a serious dilemma for many segments of the ethnic groups. Jews, for instance, wished to remain a distinct ethnic and religious group, but, like the Poles and Italians, they wanted to be and to be considered by the general community as full-fledged members of the American society and the American nation.

"Unity in Diversity"

The theory of "cultural pluralism," developed principally by Horace M. Kallen, offered the most attractive solution to this dilemma. Accepting the existence of a mainstream American culture, Kallen maintained that the dominant culture would benefit from coexistence and constant interaction with the cultures of the ethnic groups. Kallen stressed that he was not advocating the multicultural antonomous pattern of the Austro-Hungarian Empire. On the contrary, he repeatedly used the term "unity in diversity." The various ethnic groups would accept and cherish the *common* elements of American cultural, political, and social mores as represented by the public schools, but they would by their own efforts support supplemental education for their young to preserve their ethnic cultural awareness and values.

The recent re-emergence of strong ethnic loyalties in a number of white ethnic groups, the passage by Congress of the 1973 Ethnic Heritage Studies Bill, make it necessary to clarify the terms and concepts used in the discussion of ethnic or multi-cultural studies to be introduced into our schools. It seems especially important to be clear about the historical origin and the correct meaning of the concepts and theories of Americanization, the Melting Pot, and Cultural Pluralism.

Ethnic studies have a place in the curriculum of our schools, especially where parents and children demand their introduction. But it makes little sense for some spokesmen of the ethnic groups to deny, in 1976, the existence of a mainstream American culture. Monsignor Geno Baroni, a leader in the movement for the introduction of ethnic studies in schools and universities, commented in connection with the passage by Congress of the Ethnic Heritage Studies Bill that the new "program is the first significant step taken by the federal government in recognizing the necessity for a pluralistic education in our society." Father Baroni may be doing harm to his cause. Instead of modestly asking that in those areas in the country, mostly in a number of big cities, where the concentration of ethnic groups is large and cohesive, carefully prepared ethnic studies be introduced and experimented with, Monsignor Baroni assumes that America is, or is becoming, a multi-ethnic society. It is easy to predict that unless ethnic spokesmen adopt a more modest stance, the Ethnic Heritage Studies Bill will not be re-funded by Congress. It seems essential to acknowledge the existence of a mainstream American culture, which, *because* the melting pot was basically successful, is not an Anglo-Saxon culture but an American culture. This American culture rests on the bedrock of Anglo-Saxon traditions in language, law, and lore, but it has been greatly modified and enriched by infusions from many immigrant cultures. Today, that mainstream culture is so secure that it can easily afford and would probably benefit from the endeavors of some ethnic groups to preserve their own cultural heritage and values. But as Senator Richard Scheiker, of Pennsylvania, the author of the Ethnic Heritage Studies Bill stated on the floor of the Senate, the objective of his bill was to unite and not to divide America.

Kallen's slogan, unity in diversity, is as important today as it was forty years ago. There is no evidence that America is in the process of becoming a multi-ethnic society. Neither is there reason to believe that the United States may develop into another Austro-Hungarian Empire, or that bilingualism and multi-culturalism may create for us the problems that plague Belgium and Canadian Quebec. The many millions of ethnically aware Americans will probably continue their efforts to preserve their language, cultural heritage, and values, but they will do so in the frame of reference of the great changes that occurred in the eighty years that have elapsed since the period of great immigration. In the course of these decades, America, while generously allowing for the existence of separate minority groups, has become one nation.

2

The New Ethnicity and the Story of the Major Immigrant Groups

For many years, stressing ethnic separateness was frowned upon in the American society. This was true in politics, in literature and arts, and particularly in schools. Native dress, German, Yiddish, or Russian accents, or the Italian mode of speech were ridiculed in humor magazines and by comedians on the stage and radio.

Immigrants and their children were expected to learn to speak the American language properly, to dress and behave according to the established American patterns, and to cherish American institutions and established American heroes, particularly Washington, Jefferson, and Lincoln. Often, native Americans expected the immigrants to extoll America as the best and greatest country in the world. Criticism of the United States by an immigrant would usually evoke the response, "If you don't like it here, why don't you go back to where you came from?" Observing some of their relatives and friends grow rich and influential, immigrants looked on America as a land of great opportunity for economic and social advancement. Immigrants, especially those who came from economically depressed countries of central and southern Europe, acknowledged and readily accepted the domination of the Anglo-Saxon Protestants in American business, politics, and society.

Gradually, however, since the rise of Hitler and Mussolini, the dismemberment of the British Empire, and the rise of free countries in Asia and Africa, a crisis of confidence developed in Western Europe and in America. The assassination of President Kennedy, Vietnam, and growing crime and economic instability contributed to disillusionment with the Anglo-Saxon or WASP leadership, the WASP ethic and culture.

The decline of the importance and influence of Anglo-Saxon elements in American political, economic, and social life has resulted in the increased cohesiveness and influence of the white ethnic groups, which are overwhelmingly non-Protestant. The diminished status of the Anglo-Saxon Protestants has provided the opportunity for ethnics to move into positions of importance in many areas of political and economic life of the country.

As a result of the increased militancy of white ethnic minorities, the old established supremacy of the Anglo-Saxon elements of the American society in politics, education, and literature (but not in the economy) is being seriously challenged. Professor Henry May devotes the first pages of his book, *The End of American Innocence*, to a description of a dinner given by Harper Brothers in New York, on March 3, 1912, in honor of William Dean Howells, the most prominent literary figure of the time. He was honored on his seventy-fifth birthday, and the guest speaker was President William Howard Taft. Among the 400 guests were Ida Tarbell, Herbert Croly, Oswald Garrison Villard, Charles Francis Adams, Ogden Mills Reid, Alfred Mahan, the writer Winston Churchill, and James Branch Cabell. Letters were read from Thomas Hardy and Henry James. In his speech, Howells spoke of his acquaintance with Nathaniel Hawthorne, Ralph Waldo Emerson, Artemus

Ward, Harriet Beecher Stowe, Francis Parkman, Walt Whitman, Mark Twain, and others. The *New York Times* noted the next day: "Nearly everyone in the hall knew everyone else." And well they might, since this was a nearly homogeneous Anglo-Saxon Protestant group. Abraham Cahan, the editor of the Yiddish *Forward*, and a well-known writer, must have felt quite ill at ease at this WASP gathering.

If in 1976, sixty-four years later, the publishing house that sponsored the Howells dinner decided to invite 400 writers and intellectuals to honor the memory of Edmund Wilson, the recently departed distinguished critic and writer, the list of the invited guests would undoubtedly include James Dickey, John Updike, William Buckley, Jr., Mary McCarthy, William Styron, Gore Vidal, Truman Capote, but also Saul Bellow, Philip Roth, Bernard Malamud, Irving Kristol, Norman Mailer, Herman Wouk, Ralph Ellison, and James Baldwin. Jason Epstein, the editor of the *New York Review of Books*, would be on the guest list, as would Norman Podhoretz, the editor of the *Commentary*. Some spokesmen for ethnic groups would consider the contrast between the two events significant enough to cite it as evidence of the decline of Anglo-Saxon Protestant domination. They would express no regret at this development. In fact, the clear implication would be "good riddance."

Dean Leonard Chrobot of Saint Mary's College, in Orchard Lake, Michigan, would probably see in the dinner a confirmation of his view that America is moving away from the Anglo-Saxon pattern and becoming a multi-ethnic society. "American Chauvinism is dying," Father Chrobot said in his testimony. "Yankee ethnocentrism, which believes in the inherent superiority of its own group, and looks with contempt on other cultures, must be finally buried." The comments of Chrobot on this complex issue are rather routine and superficial, but Michael Novak's careful analysis in *The Rise of the Unmeltable Ethnics* of the deep schism and contradictions between the WASP ethic and the structure of value and belief of the sons and grandsons of immigrants from central and southern Europe, deserves serious consideration. Almost painfully, but with a sense of profound relief, Novak confesses that he and his fellow ethnics have a negative gut reaction to the fundamental tenets of what he defines as the Anglo-Saxon credo. They resent and reject the WASP ideal of success as a worthwhile goal of life and doubt the ability of the American society to transform its members and especially immigrants into better people deeply committed to individual and national progress. The ethnics, Novak tells us, do not want "to keep cool," and they resent the Puritan preference for self-restraint over the free expression of emotions. Moral indignation at occasional violence, corruption, and other evidence of basic human weaknesses is alien to them. In fact, Novak says that "Protestant-American myths of success and self-help required the immigrants to change their conception of themselves, their families and society." He is delighted that in this age of militant ethnicity, the ethnics (and he joyfully includes himself) can finally throw off these restraints and be themselves.

Novak berates the American Catholic Church, which, in his view, is ruled by Irish bishops who have accepted the WASP values of order, calm, and rationality and have imposed on the ethnic groups a Catholic worship that leaves the worshippers unfulfilled and resentful. The central European and the southern European immigrants and many of their descendants believe, Novak tells us, in a *pagan* Catholicism with its stress on religious processions, mystery ceremonies, and an unabashed worship of the Madonna. "The Irish are pagans like the Slavs, the Italians and the Greeks," according to Novak, "but pagans who have allowed their church to make Christianity an agent of order and cleanliness rather than an agent of mystery, ghostliness, fear, terror and passion, which at its best it was."

At first glance, there may be some attraction in this plea for a more passionate, more meaningful religious experience, but the "pagan" Catholicism of pre-war Poland,

Lithuania, Slovakia, and other places in Europe had its dark and bloody side, which Novak chooses to ignore. A large measure of superstition and an even larger measure of intolerance were built into this version of Catholic faith.

"Pagan" Catholicism in central and southern Europe made no distinction between nationality and religion, and Catholicism in many of the countries of central and southern Europe was *the* religion. It meant that all instruction in elementary schools and gymnasia (the high schools) began with the recitation of the Lord's Prayer during which the non-Catholic boys and girls in class were required to stand at attention while their Catholic peers stood with their hands folded in a required stance. Obviously, the non-Catholic children had a feeling of alienation. Novak's apotheosis of that ancient, passionate but thoroughly intolerant Catholicism needs some thoughtful analysis.

The American Catholic Church has accepted many reforms and is experiencing a profound upheaval, which only its communicants can judge and evaluate. But the Catholic Church operating under the principle of separation of church and state, in a country with a Protestant majority, can well be lauded and not condemned for stressing rationality, self-restraint, and tolerance.

Novak's plea for a freer rein on emotions is not limited to religion. It extends to other aspects of life: "The Anglo-Saxon fears overpopulation and crowding. . . . Not so the Italian, the Slav, the Spaniard, the Greek. Southern and Eastern Europeans have a far more 'pagan' attitude to life." Even for those who have some reservations about the Anglo-Saxons and their airs of superiority, the WASP ethic looks surprisingly attractive when contrasted with the "pagan Catholic ethic" of Novak and his allies. At least in the former, there is a chance of making it, in reasonable health and security, to a reasonably old age. Of course, Novak would argue, as he has, that non-WASPs can make it in our society only on the terms laid down by the WASP-dominated society.

Virtually no word has a more sinister connotation in Novak's vocabulary than "Americanization." The same is true of most of the vocal ethnic spokesmen. Novak merely articulates more clearly and more frankly the theme repeated in speeches of many ethnic leaders, that to Poles, Slavs, Serbs, Italians, and others, Americanization has meant that they were "catechized, cajoled and condescended to by quadrons of good Anglo-Saxon attitudes. . . . The entire experience of becoming American is summarized in the experience of being made to feel guilty."

Dr. Rudolph Vecoli, Professor of History at the University of Minnesota and President of the American-Italian Historical Association, stated in his testimony before Congressman Pucinski's committee that Americanization, which he termed "forcible assimilation," was a dismal failure. He compared the effort to prepare the immigrants for the passing of the naturalization examinations to the efforts of the Germans to Germanize the Poles or the efforts of the Hungarians to Magyarize the Slovaks. "Americanization" is used by ethnic spokesmen as a synonym for the "melting pot idea," and is considered an effort to deprive the immigrants and their descendants of their pride and knowledge of their ethnic roots and heritage.

Many of the political and the intellectual leaders of the ethnic groups are gleefully proclaiming the failure of the melting pot theory. The continued existence of the ethnic groups and their militant reawakening are cited as decisive proof of the demise of the melting pot myth.

Ethnic leaders proclaim, to the delight of their audiences, the end of the pre-eminence of the WASPs in America. They paint a picture of the American society as stricken by a variety of afflictions, including the questioning of long established moral values, the decline in patriotism, a growing disunity, and the alienation of the young. All these are allegedly the result of the misguided emphasis on WASP values, of the suppression of ethnic differences, and of the attempt to "homogenize" America. The salvation is seen in a return to the ethnic roots.

The rise of often fierce ethnic loyalties among many millions of descendants of immigrant groups is related to their fears, dilemmas, and unfulfilled aspirations. These

differ from group to group but all of them can be understood only upon the background of the history and the
nature of their original immigration into the United States.
To look to history as a source of enlightenment for a complex contemporary societal phenomenon has not been
popular in recent years. History and the teaching of history
have been under intense attack. Many would have us believe that Voltaire, a brilliant historian, was serious when
he made his flippant remark: "History is the tricks we play
on the dead."

Some social scientists argue that history has little or
nothing to teach us about contemporary affairs, while the
social sciences like sociology and political science address
themselves to the solution of some of the most vexing contemporary societal issues. The state of affairs in our country and in the world today lends only limited support to
the assertion that history offers no help. Whatever the
broader ramifications of this dispute between the historians and the social scientists may be, the present status
and the problems of the major white ethnic groups in
America cannot be understood without a long backward
look at their respective histories. To a large extent, it is
the nature and the story of their original mass immigrations to America that determined their present status and
even their future.

The Italian-Americans

The problems and dilemmas faced by Italian-Americans
today can be understood only by reference to the peculiar
history of Italian immigration into the United States. The
immigration from Italy came between 1880 and 1910. In
that relatively short period of thirty years, 4.5 million Italians came to America. They came almost exclusively from
southern Italy, mainly from the island of Sicily and from
the regions of Abruzzi, Calabria, and Campania. In the
course of history, Sicily was governed by Greeks, Cartha-
ginians, Romans, Vandals, Arabs, Spaniards, Austrians,
Frenchmen, and others. To survive, the Sicilian peasants
had to learn to hate, ignore, and outfox their rulers and to

distrust all levels of authority. The only entities that mattered were the family and the village. Only in the love and solidarity of the "famiglia" (the immediate family and all the "blood" relatives) could one eke out a living and have a measure of security in a hostile environment. Beyond the family was the loose association of the villages; beyond that, all was enemy territory.

The Sicilian and other southern Italian immigrants to America were overwhelmingly peasants, *contadini*, and artisans, *artigiani*, who came from the poorest regions of Italy in order to escape poverty and exploitation. But unlike the millions of Jews who immigrated to the United States almost at the same time from the wretched villages of Poland, Russia, Lithuania, and Hungary, the Italian peasants loved their sun-baked villages, and many of them longed to return. Some had no desire to settle in America permanently. They worked hard in the land of Columbus, saved as much money as they could and then returned to their villages as "rich" Americans.

Between 1908 and 1916, several hundred thousand Italians returned to their native land. The publicity given to this exodus of Italians to the Old Country was greeted with anger by the American press and public. The ridiculed "dagos," "wops," the "leftovers of Southern Italy," were now accused of ingratitude to America, of exploiting the economic opportunity that this country gave them and taking their newly acquired resources back to their country of origin. The nativists and the xenophobes had added ammunition for their constant attacks on the "uncouth" and "uncivilized" immigrants.

The adjustment of this mass of southern Italians to America would have been difficult even without the added handicaps of animosity and ridicule. They were mostly illiterate workers who could only do unskilled labor. They worked hard and were paid little, building railroads and toiling on construction jobs. Even those among them who were skilled masons, bricklayers, and stonecutters were exploited by the *padrones*, their own labor bosses. The *padrone* was a job contractor who recruited the workers and dealt with the American employers. Many of the *padrones* were ruthless exploiters of their compatriots while others helped them to find their way in the new environment.

Faced with these enormous difficulties in a strange and largely hostile environment, the Italian immigrants made every effort to hold on to their old ways of life, to preserve the elaborate mores of the "la famiglia." To do that, they settled in closely knit Italian neighborhoods, which they considered essential to their spiritual comfort, peace of mind, and even survival. In New York, they lived on Mulberry Street, and on Tenth Avenue in a "Little Italy," in St. Louis they settled in "Dago Hill," and in other cities their settlements were known as "Woptowns" and "Macaroni Hills." In 1887, the *Chicago Herald* complained of the "nasty and cheap living" in Chicago's Little Italy, in the area bordered by Halstead, Polk, and 12th streets.

In these sealed off enclaves, Sicilian Italians guarded their complex system of family, social, and religious relations developed over centuries of the turbulent history of their island. The solidarity of the family and strict familial loyalty were constantly stressed. The values and customs and the rigid "honor code" were used to preserve their families from disintegration and to resist the onslaught of precipitous assimilation of the young into the Anglo-Saxon culture and environment. To counteract the enormous pull of the American environment and the attraction of opportunities for success and advancement in the outside world, Italian immigrant parents ridiculed the world of the Yankees and often did all they legally could to limit the years of school attendance. Italian boys were encouraged to go to work as early as possible to add to the family's income and the girls were taken out of school at the end of the legally mandated school attendance. Public schools were considered by many Italian immigrant families as breeding grounds of atheism and immorality.

The life of the immigrants centered around the family and the church. While the men remained cynical and disdainful of the clergy, as only devout Italians can be, for

the women and children the church was the center of their
lives. The church was important, but it was the larger
family that was the source of comfort and security to immigrants suffering from pangs of severe culture shock.
Sundays, particularly, were divided almost equally between
church and family.

Mario Puzo, in *The Fortunate Pilgrim,* a brilliant novel
centering on the life of the new Italian immigrant families,
describes a New York street in "Little Italy" on a Sunday
afternoon:

> Tenth Avenue open all the way to the river at Twelfth
> with no intervening wall to give shade, was lighter than
> other avenues in the city and hotter during the day. Now
> it was deserted. The enormous midday Sunday feast would
> last to four o'clock, what with nuts and wine and telling
> of family legends. Some people were visiting more fortun-
> ate relatives who had achieved success and moved to their
> own homes on Long Island and New Jersey. Others used
> the day for attending funerals, weddings, christenings, or
> most important of all—bringing cheer and food to sick rela-
> tives in Bellevue.

But the process of assimilation to America, while slow, continued relentlessly. Italians who moved to New Jersey and
to Long Island, while remaining a separate ethnic group,
were rapidly assimilating the mores and customs of the
dominant American society. The same was true of many
Italians who moved to California, where they went into
fruit and vegetable farming in the coastal and valley areas,
settling in large numbers in Los Angeles and San Francisco. Fishing, restaurants, and construction became virtual Italian monopolies in many parts of California. In San
Francisco, Dominico Ghirardelli was a famous chocolate
manufacturer and merchant, and Ghirardelli Square on
San Francisco's waterfront is today a magnificent arcade
of shops and restaurants. The most outstanding success
story of an Italian immigrant was that of Amadeo Pietro
(known as A. P.) Giannini, a merchant and real estate
broker, who founded the Bank of America in the North
Beach section, then San Francisco's "Little Italy." Today,

the Bank of America has branches all over California and is one of the largest banking firms in America.

Things were much more complex on the Eastern Seaboard and in the Middle West, especially in Chicago, where many Italian immigrants worked in the two great clothing firms, Hart Schaffner and Marx and L. B. Kuppenheimer. It is to Chicago that the first connection between Italians and crime activities can be traced. It is not surprising that in the society of Sicilian immigrants who were despised and ridiculed by the dominant society and who were forced into underpaid and unskilled jobs, a small minority turned to crime as a route to economic and social advancement. The ethnic cohesion and group loyalty of the Sicilians, their traditional hostility and suspicion of all levels of government and authority, helped gang leaders like James Colossimo, John Torio, and Al Capone to conduct their criminal operations. These activities were greatly facilitated by the corrupt conditions of Chicago politics. In fact, it must be said that some of the downtrodden immigrants, the people called "Dagos" and "Wops," felt a measure of pride in the swaggering "feudal baron of Cicero," Al Capone, who treated important political figures in Chicago with contempt and who for many years was an untouchable as far as the law was concerned. Time and again Capone was heard boasting that he "owned" the Chicago police. Humbert S. Nelli wrote in *Italians in Chicago* that

> Under the leadership of John Torio and his successor, Capone, Italians exerted a powerful economic and political influence in Chicago, and made a spectacular and notorious entrance into the mainstream of city life. . . . Their glittering successes and extravagant excesses, and the extensive publicity accorded their actions by the press, diverted public attention from the widespread but less sensational accomplishments of Chicago's law-abiding Italians.

For some boys in the "Little Italies" across the country, the crime syndicate offered an opportunity to gain some self-respect and achieve relative economic security. This was especially true in Chicago, where criminal gangs abounded.

A high official in the Illinois state government, a respected Italian-American leader who grew up in Chicago's
"Little Italy," related that "there were only two ways for
the boys in my neighborhood to get up the greasy pole of
success. Either through hard work and education, which
took longer or through service to the various crime 'families', which took less time and paid quick returns but was
dangerous. I took the road of education and honest work."
And yet, he added, "I can easily be charged with having
links to the Syndicate. This is a very tricky business. Of
course, I know crime syndicate figures. I played with them
in the streets of the First Ward, went to the same church
and often dated the same girls. If I were to go to a wedding
of a daughter of one of my boyhood pals, I may well be
charged with having 'connections with the Mafia.'" Many
law-abiding Italian-Americans across the country are faced
with this dilemma.

The Jews

The contrast between the history of Italian and Jewish
mass immigrations and the way in which this history has
shaped the respective destinies of Italian-Americans and
Jewish-Americans is great indeed. Largely because of their
different pasts, the Italian and Jewish communities in
America today face different problems and dilemmas. Ap-
proximately in the same period of the great Italian immigrations, 1880-1914, over 3 million Jews came to America,
mostly from Russia, Poland, Lithuania, and Hungary.

Unlike the Italians, the Jews were not peasants. In fact,
they were not allowed to own land in the countries of their
origin. They came from cities and towns (*shtetlech*),
where they had lived in ghettos or segregated and restricted areas. Governmental restrictions forced them to
make their livelihood as small merchants, peddlers, and
artisans. But a respectable proportion of the Jewish immigrants were doctors, engineers, writers, journalists,
teachers, and students.

Unlike the Italians, even the masses of the poor and
destitute Jews were not illiterate. They spoke and read

Yiddish and Hebrew, and many Jewish intellectuals spoke, read, and wrote Russian, Polish, German, and English. Their flight from Russia and Poland was a flight not only from poverty but also from religious persecution. Many Jewish intellectuals and students were socialists or Zionists, and they fled from political persecution of the Czarist police.

Unlike many Italian or Polish immigrants, the Jews came to America to stay. They had no love and less nostalgia for the cities and towns and villages of Russia and Poland where they lived as an oppressed and persecuted minority. The sad parting of the Jews from the mythical village of Anatevka in *Fiddler on the Roof* is a theatrical hyperbole, not a historical truth. On the contrary, as the Jews disembarked in New York, they wanted to forget their life and experiences in Europe as soon as possible, and they were determined to become American citizens as quickly as the law would allow.

Enrollment in the citizenship classes, which Leo Rosten made famous in *The Education of H*Y*M*A*N* K*A*P-*L*A*N*, was one of the first steps taken by the Jewish immigrants upon their arrival. Among the Jews it was a *mitzvah*, almost a religious good deed, to become a citizen and vote in the elections. Since they were basically literate, they had little difficulty in meeting the legal requirements for citizenship.

Unlike the Italians, the Jews did not regard America, with its unique ways of life, as a threat, and they experienced less cultural shock than the Italians or the Poles. To millions of Jewish immigrants, America was the land of their dreams and hopes. It was the hope of immigration to America, where they often had relatives already residing, that made the misery of their lives in the *shtetlech* of Russia and Poland bearable. They read the letters from their American relatives with wonder and anticipation. To be sure, the reality of New York's crowded and dirty East Side tenement houses was different from the New York of their dreams, but America still was a marvelous haven of refuge. It was for the Jews a land of freedom and oppor-

tunity, after centuries of wandering and oppression across
Europe as a despised minority, doomed to suffering for
their religious beliefs. Where else in 2,000 years of wan-
derings had they heard at every public meeting that this
was "the land of the free."

The Jews were, of course, also somewhat bewildered
by the new American environment, especially in huge,
bustling New York. But they had one great advantage
over the Italians, the Poles, the Russians, and the Slovaks.
They were familiar with urban living, and they had centuries of experience of moving from one country to another
and of having to adjust to new environments, new cultures,
and new governments. They had learned how to live among
Russians, Poles, Lithuanians, and Hungarians, and how to
still remain a separate entity. They came from countries
where they were a minority, and they knew how to accept
the advantages and disadvantages of this status. In their
countries of origin, the Jews, by their own decision and by
the will of the majority of the population, were not Russians,
Poles, Hungarians, or Lithuanians, but Jews. They neither
particularly wanted nor were given the rights of citizenship
in the countries of their habitation. But the attitude of the
Jewish immigrants to the United States was entirely different. Here all men were equal, at least, under the law,
and here they were safe from political and religious persecution.

To the Italians and the Poles, manifestations of xeno-
phobia, of Anglo-Saxon nativism, were a shocking and de-
meaning experience. For Jewish newcomers in America to
be called "kikes" or "sheenies" was old stuff. They had
seen much, much worse. In Russia, their worry was not
insulting remarks but pogroms. Unlike the Italians and
the Poles, Jews accumulated a great deal of know-how in
dealing with outside hostility or discrimination and were
ready to cope with its relatively mild manifestations in
America. They became, in the course of time, experts
in survival in hostile environments. They knew how to
ignore occasional anti-Semitic or nativist propaganda and
reveled in the atmosphere of freedom and in the almost

unlimited opportunities offered by the new country. They welcomed the pluralistic character of the American society, rejoiced in its often proclaimed egalitarianism, and cheerfully disregarded or discounted the ridicule and hostility that they sometimes encountered. The contrast of how they were treated in government offices, in post offices, in courts, on railroads, and in schools in Russia and in America was startling and deeply gratifying.

Jewish immigrants were happy that the new country adhered to the principle of separation of church and state. In Russia, where the Orthodox Church was virtually identical with the state, and priests were government officials, and in Poland where Polish nationalism and Polish Roman Catholicism were intrinsically bound together, Jews suffered both as a national and as a religious minority. The contrast with America could not have been greater. The lack of officially sanctioned class distinction in America made upward social mobility much easier. The clear class distinctions between the landed nobility and the peasants in Russia and Poland, forced the Jews to act as middlemen between the two groups with the consequences of becoming the scapegoats of both the big landowners and of the exploited peasants. This was especially true in times of economic depression or of a political crisis.

In a short time, Jews became unabashed patriots and boosters of America. Jewish radicals, socialists, Bundists, and the Jewish communists, hated the inequalities of the capitalist system, but they too loved America where they were not shadowed by secret agents, where they were free to speak and to write, and where they were not living under the threat of jail or exile. Jews, as their affluence was growing, became convinced that America was truly a *Goldene Medine*, a Golden Land of freedom and opportunity.

The editor of the Yiddish *Daily Forward*, Abraham Cahan explains the attraction of America to the Jewish immigrants in his novel, *The Rise of David Levinsky*. During an evening concert in a resort in the Catskill mountains in upper New York State, a conductor of a small

orchestra had a hard time rousing his audience, composed
almost completely of recent immigrants, from the stupor
induced by the heavy meal. Selections from *Aida*, from
popular Broadway hits, and from Jewish musicals all fell
flat. The audience remained drowsy and apathetic. In
desperation, the band struck up *The Star-Spangled Banner*.
Cahan writes,

> The effect was overwhelming. The few hundred diners
> rose like one man, applauding. The children and many of
> the adults caught up the tune joyously, passionately. . . .
> Men and women were offering thanksgiving to the flag
> under which they were eating this good dinner, wearing
> these expensive clothes. There was the jingle of newly-
> acquiring dollars in our applause. But there was something
> else in it as well. Many of those who were now paying
> tribute to the Stars and Stripes were listening to the tune
> with grave, solemn mien. It was as if they were saying:
> "We are not persecuted under this flag. At last we have
> found a home."

The uniqueness of the Jewish experience as immigrants
to America had its effect not only on the first generation
but also on the second and third generations of Jews.
Many of second and third or even fourth generation of
American Italians and Polish-Americans carry with them
the memory, bequeathed to them by their parents and
grandparents, of the old days of suffering, of ridicule and
discrimination. These accounts are still bound to rankle
and to affect ethnic attitudes. By and large, that is not
true of the present generation of American Jews. Its members remember the tales of steady progress and of the
ever-greater measure of economic success attained in the
United States by their grandparents or parents. On the
whole, these are tales of hardships and hard work but it
is also the story of years filled with progress and fulfilled
hopes for a better life.

The key to the success of the Jewish immigrants was
education. When Jewish parents themselves lacked general
education, or when their education was limited to Hebrew
or Yiddish studies, they more than made up for it by their

zeal for the education of their children. The desired goal
was not, as it was in most Italian families, a high school
diploma, but a college degree. There is some truth in the
myth that all Jewish mothers wanted their children to become doctors or lawyers—and many did. Passion for learning and a strong belief that education was the best road
to advancement were probably the most important characteristics of the massive Jewish immigration to America.

This appreciation for knowledge and dedication to
learning and study did not spring up suddenly on the
American soil. It developed directly from the long tradition of the study of the Torah and the Talmud by generations of young Jews in many lands of dispersion. The
most respected men in the *shtetlech* were not the rich men
but the scholars. No wonder that in America, where educational opportunities were open to their children, the
public schools were almost fanatically supported by Jewish
parents. Schools and teachers always enjoyed the strong
backing of the Jewish community. Many young Jews in
New York, Chicago, and other big cities went into the
teaching profession and, taking advantage of a merit system that provided for advancement through examinations,
they quickly occupied positions of importance as principals
and district superintendents. Others graduated from free
universities like the City College of New York and went
on to become doctors, lawyers, professors, and businessmen.

In contrast, few Italian children of the second generation went to college. As we have seen, there was often no
encouragement from the Italian family—on the contrary,
many Italian immigrant parents pressured their children to
leave the alien public school at the earliest legal age and
get jobs to add to the family's income. Many of these jobs
were in the police, fire, and sanitation departments of large
cities, in the post offices, and in the electric and telephone
companies. Italians seldom occupied top positions in industry or commerce and many remained in blue-collar jobs,
particularly in the construction industry.

Of course, not all Jewish immigrants or their children

went to colleges and to professions. Many found employment in the clothing industry. "Jewish immigrants," writes
Moses Rischin in *The Promised City*, "separated by religious proscriptions, customs, language from the surround-
ing city, found a place in the clothing industry, where the
initial shock of contact with a bewildering world was
tempered by a familiar milieu." In time, the center of the
clothing industry in New York became dominated by Jews.
Jewish clothing workers were primarily responsible for the
founding of the Amalgamated Clothing Workers of America
and of the International Ladies Garment Workers Union.
After an initial period of bitter strikes, collective bargaining
and mediation of disputes became the established practice
in the clothing industry and it was soon widely imitated in
other industries. Significantly, since most of the owners of
the clothing factories in New York and Chicago were Jews,
as were most of the workers and almost all of the union
leaders, "the bosses" were subject to an effective pressure
from the generally liberal Jewish community which sym-
pathized with the demands of the workers for a living
wage and better and safer working conditions.

Today, there are few Jewish workers left in the clothing industry, although some of the leaders of the Amalgamated and of the I.L.G.W. and of the hatters and fur workers unions, as well as many of the factory owners and
clothing manufacturers, are Jews. In contrast to the Italians
and Poles, Jews moved out from the blue-collar jobs with
great rapidity.

The Poles

The pattern of Polish mass immigration to the United
States was significantly different from that of the Jewish
and Italian immigrations, and these differences have also
shaped the particular structure and the unique problems
facing American Poles today. The most significant fact to
remember is that Poles who came to this country in large
numbers between the years 1880 and 1910 did not come
from a free sovereign homeland. In fact, there was no
Poland on the map of Europe after 1795. In 1795, after

800 years of existence as an independent state, Poland was a strong and distinct national entity. The Poles, who had accepted Christianity in the ninth century, considered themselves the defenders of the Roman Catholic faith and an outpost of Western Christian civilization against the repeated onslaughts of the Russians, the Turks, the Mongols, the Tartars, and other "heretic" invaders. Poles proudly claimed that Poland was a living "Christian Wall" against the conquest of Europe. Polish children were taught on their fathers' knees the story of the heroic contributions of King Jan Sobieski and his Polish army who helped defeat the Turks in 1683 at the gates of Vienna. Poles also cherished the memory of their resistance to the repeated invasions by the Teutonic Knights who came from East Prussia and the victories they attained in preserving their independence against the invading armies of Sweden and Russia.

For centuries, Poland's powerful neighbors were determined not to allow the Poles to live as an independent people. Finally, in 1795, Russia occupied eastern Poland, Prussia took the western and northern lands, and the southern part of Poland was incorporated into Austria. From that time on, for 125 years, Poles were ruled by three foreign powers. They regained their independence in 1918, when a free Poland was created by the terms of the Treaty of Versailles, based on the Wilsonian principle of self-determination of nations.

This long period of partition of Poland and the incessant struggle of Poles for independence, marked by great uprisings and rebellions in 1831 and 1863, had a lasting and profound influence on the Polish people. They became one of the most nationalistic and patriotic peoples in Europe. To the Poles, who had lost their independence to foreign invaders and who were determined to regain their freedom, love of country became almost a national obsession. The Polish poet, Adam Mickiewicz, put it well in verse in one of his poems: "My fatherland, you are like health, only those who have lost you, can know your value." It was indeed a desperate struggle that the

Polish people waged against the might of Czarist Russia,
the military machine of Prussia, and the immense power
of the Austro-Hungarian Empire. The occupying powers
attempted in varying degrees to suppress the spirit of
Polish nationalism through forced Russification or German-
ization, through bribery and political concessions, and often by brutal force.

All these efforts failed. The Poles had no independent
political institutions, their military rebellions were sup-
pressed, their sons died on foreign battlefields, in the vain
hope of enlisting sympathy and military aid in the fight
for an independent Poland. But their dedication to the idea
of a free Poland never faltered. If anything, during the
period of foreign domination, the Poles became an even
more united people—united by the will for independence
and united in one language and culture and in one religious
faith. The Polish language became a precious and effective bond for Poles in all three sectors of occupation.
To speak Polish, to write in Polish, to love the Polish
language became an almost religious commandment for
all Poles. The patriotic poetry of the great Polish poets,
Adam Mickiewicz, Julius Slowacki, and the Messianic writings of Stanislaw Wyspianski became not only great literature for educated Poles, but their most sacred treasure
and a source of constant inspiration.

For the mass of poor and largely illiterate peasants
who formed the overwhelming majority of the population,
the spirit of Polish nationalism was kept alive by the Polish
Catholic Church. While the Catholic Church in Poland was
faithful and obedient to Rome, it was primarily a *Polish*
Catholic Church; it supported the fierce Polish nationalism
and kept the devotion to the Polish language, Polish customs, and Polish hopes and aspirations for independence.
Priests delivered patriotic sermons in Polish, and religious
schools taught Polish language and literature, often in the
face of dire threats by the occupying authorities. As time
went on, the lines of demarcation between Polish nationalism and Polish Catholicism became blurred, and they remain blurred until the present time.

Several million Poles came to America during the period
of the occupation of their country by foreign powers, and
they brought with them both the spirit of fierce Polish nationalism and an unbounded devotion to the Polish Catholic
Church. In that, they differed from the Italians, who came
from a free Italy, and especially from Sicilians who had
little comprehension or feeling for Italian nationalism and
who, while devout Catholics, viewed the Italian Church
and Italian priests with a great deal of suspicion, if not
outright cynicism. Obviously, the contrast with the Jews,
who felt little if any allegiance to the countries of their
origin, was even greater. Polish nationalism and special
devotion to the Catholic Church are still the most outstanding characteristics of those American Poles who have preserved their ethnic identity. Polish nationalism, however,
constitutes no conflict with their strong patriotic devotion
to the United States of America.

Poles have had significant ties with America since
colonial times. Poles were in the Jamestown colony and
two Polish officers, Thaddeus Kosciuszko and Casimir
Pulaski, were heroes of the American Revolution. General
Kosciuszko distinguished himself in the Battle of Saratoga
and fortified West Point which was General George Washington's headquarters. Pulaski became a Brigadier General
in the Revolutionary Army and died in a gallant cavalry
charge during the siege of Savannah.

But the mass of Polish immigration came, as we have
said, in the last two decades of the 19th century and in the
period before World War I. It was overwhelmingly peasant
in character. During that period of time over three million
Poles came to America, paralleling the massive Italian and
Jewish immigrations. While the special character of these
immigration waves has influenced the nature of the Italian-
American and Jewish-American communities, a case can
be made that the status, the image, and the problems of
the contemporary Polish community, or of Polonia, as
Poles call it, reflect the unique history of the original
Polish immigration in bolder and clearer relief. In com-
parison with the Italians, the Jews, or the Irish, Poles have

made less economic and social progress in the American milieu. The reason for this phenomenon has, of course, nothing to do with the innate abilities of Poles, but is related to the point at which they started their journey to the New World.

Polish immigrants were mostly peasants who came from an occupied country, and from a society which still practiced a variation of feudal economy. Professor Florian Znaniecki estimated that 60 percent of Polish immigrants were landless peasants who eked out a bare living as hired hands on large estates and 27 percent were small landowners. Polish immigration included very few skilled workers or artisans. The mass of the Polish peasants who came to the United States had no skills to survive in the industrialized and strange country to which they came. They spoke rudimentary, peasants' Polish and were overwhelmingly illiterate both in their own language and in English. Thus, unlike the Jewish immigrants and to some extent the Italian newcomers, most Poles were not able to benefit in their adjustment period from reading the few Polish newspapers in America. In addition, unlike the Jews who were experienced international travelers, and unlike the Italians who benefitted from the love and glamor that American society has always accorded Italy, Poles came from a country which was in chains and which was unknown to Americans.

All that Poles had to offer America was their inordinate capacity and willingness to do hard physical labor. This contribution should have been accepted with gratitude by the booming American economy and industry but in fact Poles were shown little compassion and even less appreciation. Bewildered in the new society Polish immigrants were determined to adjust and to survive. To do this, they became laborers in the steel mills of Pittsburgh and Gary, in the automobile factories in Detroit, and in the stockyards of Chicago. Some Poles who had experience in the coal mines in Poland, and many others who did not, went to work, under hard and dangerous conditions, in the coal fields of Pennsylvania.

No work was too hard, too menial, too coarse, or too dangerous for the Poles. They had no choice and could not be choosy about jobs if their families were to survive in their new environment. This hard, demanding labor was a signal contribution of these millions of brawny and healthy immigrants who without complaining or rebelling helped to make America the industrial giant it is today. There was virtually no crime among the Poles; their young people did not consider illegal activities as one possible avenue for advancement in the new, strange, and often hostile environment. Crime was unthinkable in a Polish neighborhood where the authority of the parents, of the priests, and of the police were highly respected, and where the emphasis was on hard work, thrift, and savings. Savings banks abounded, and most Polish fraternal organizations were (and are) also insurance and savings institutions.

How did America repay the contribution and the exemplary behavior of these Polish immigrants? In return, they did not receive a sense of welcome and appreciation. On the contrary, ridicule and scorn were heaped on the heads of these simple, uneducated folk who worked sixteen hours a day in dangerously insecure mines, mills, and stockyards, for pitifully small wages.

It is virtually impossible to exaggerate the severity of the cultural shock suffered by the mass of Polish peasant immigrants. They came to this country not from the advanced regions of Poland, around Warsaw, Poznan, and Lodz, but from the least advanced regions of the highlands in southern and eastern Poland. They came from isolated, primitive villages; they had no interest and no part in the management of their own affairs and no voice in the political affairs of the region or of the nation. Politics were the exclusive domain of the aristocratic landlords and of the country gentry. If they voted, they did so as the local priest or government official told them to vote. Even the rudiments of the democratic process were unknown to them.

Alexander Hertz's *Reflections on America* includes a

perceptive analysis of the situation faced by Polish immigrants:

The leap from the world of family and neighbor relationships to the world of big-city, industrial civilization of the United States, was of a fantastic dimension. This was not only a change of place, of country and of a mode of earning a living. It was something much greater—it was a transition from a way of life based on a very simple order to a new order of life, which was fluid, very complex and which used the most advanced technology. One ought to think very deeply about the dimensions of the psychological revolution, in order to evaluate properly the extent of the effort demanded of the immigrant if he were to stake roots in the new soil.

Much of what Hertz says applied also to other immigrant groups, but the difficulties confronted by the Poles in this period of transition were particularly great. They were much more severe than those experienced by the Irish immigrants, who spoke English and had considerable familiarity with Anglo-Saxon mores and institutions. Jewish immigrants were overwhelmingly literate and were becoming "Americanized" daily by the Yiddish newspapers, which devoted many pages to instructing them how to survive and to prosper in the new land. In addition, both the Jewish and the Italian immigrations included artisans and intellectuals who provided a ready pool of potential leaders and spokesmen. Poles had few of these advantages.

Children of Polish immigrants suffered in the public schools the usual tribulations of the other immigrant students, but they had to cope with another handicap—their unpronounceable names. Anglo-Saxon and Irish teachers resented the effort it took to pronounce these names correctly and often suggested to a Stankiewicz or Wroblewski to tell his parents to change his name to "Stanley" or to "Warren." Polish children soon perceived directly, or by repeated innuendo, that to get along in school you had to forget or to hide your Polish ties and identity. When they told their Polish parents, who struggled in the occupied Poland to keep their Polish language of their reluctance to speak Polish and of their desire to shorten their names, the reaction was often harsh and unyielding. No wonder then, that among many second generation Poles there developed a growing feeling of inferiority. They often suffered from the hostility of their teachers to their cultural heritage and they were ashamed of their poor and illiterate parents, who, as they soon discovered, did not even speak a "good" or literate Polish.

The generation gap was real and painful, and it had its effects on the psyche and the state of mind of American Poles. The effects are still evident today. Professor Eugene Kusielewicz, President of the Kosciuszko Foundation, maintains that even the third generation of Poles "suffers from the same feeling of inferiority that is characteristic of the rest of Polonia." This feeling of inferiority, he believes, is reinforced by the largely negative image that Poles present to the rest of America. In support of his view, Kusielewicz cites a survey made by the Polish-American writer Wieslaw Kuniczak, which found that Americans consider Polish-Americans to be "anti-Semites, narrow, simple-minded, clumsy, stupid, anti-liberal, reactionary . . . and vulgar."

Many Polish leaders dispute the views of Kusielewicz and Kuniczak and cite evidence indicating that many second and third generation Poles are interested in and are proud of their Polish identity and culture. The truth is probably that some young Polish-Americans are ashamed of their ethnic origin and others are proud of being Polish, while the attitude of the vast majority fluctuates somewhere in between these two extremes.

Historically, it is not difficult to understand the origins of the "dumb Polack" syndrome. As we have said, Polish immigrants were mostly illiterate, in Polish and in English. They had no skills and were doing menial work. They were on the lowest rung in the pecking order of employees in the mines, the steel mills, the stockyards, or small business establishments. It was often difficult for these laborers to follow the instructions of the foremen or of their bosses. Polish workers did not have the *padrones* who helped the Italian immigrants on construction or on railroad jobs. Consequently, they were thought to be unintelligent and even slow-witted. Nobody seemed to care to get to know these newcomers, and the first impression lingered into the second and third generations, which include doctors, lawyers, engineers, and professors.

In recent years, American Poles have launched a long overdue counter-offensive. They have branded their image false and the "Polish jokes" as an unworthy and an un-American abomination. In a keynote address to the 1970 National Convention of the Polish American Congress, President Aloysius Mazewski declared,

> Our most urgent task is the presentation of Polonia's image in a historically and sociologically appraised frame of reference. It is not an easy task; its difficulties are deeply rooted in the past neglect and ignorance of our own worth in the mainstream of American life.

American Poles are now fighting back against their detractors and defamers. The Polish American Congress has established a special Committee on Education and Cultural Affairs, which has demanded from the communication media the elimination of "Polish jokes" and asked them to present the contributions and the positive life-styles of the Polish community in America. So far, this campaign has only been partly successful.

There is little evidence to substantiate the widespread assumption that American Poles are more racist than any other group in America. Reliable polls of public opinion have established that the Poles are in fact less anti-black than some segments of the white Protestant Anglo-Saxon. Like most of the problems faced by American Poles, this question, too, relates to their low economic status. Poles live in low-income neighborhoods in inner cities into which blacks are trying to move to escape from the wretched slums. The other area of confrontation is the job market. Both groups compete for semi-skilled jobs, and the pressure of the blacks for admission into craft unions creates fears among the Poles who are long-time members of these unions. "The conflict between the Poles and the blacks is basically neither racial nor ideological—it is economic," said Joseph Bialasiewich, the editor of *Polonia*, a Polish weekly published in Chicago. He made this statement sitting in his office, which was once located in the heart of the Polish community in Chicago and which has now become an area with a majority of blacks and Spanish-speaking people. Most Polish institutions in Chicago are located in the Milwaukee and Division area, which has now largely been deserted by their clients, the Polish homeowners. In Detroit, the blacks and the Poles have united their efforts to raise their economic status and to fight the city's blight. They have formed a Black-Polish Conference, which has been effective in achieving better schools and better city services in the black and Polish areas of Detroit.

However, American Poles are convinced that the federal government has concentrated on helping the Negroes to achieve equal rights and a higher standard of living to the exclusion of their group, which is also in need of help. A resolution passed at the 1970 Convention of the American Polish Congress said in part:

> Be it resolved that the President of the United States be commended for his recognition of the talent and abilities of the members of our Black community by the appointment of a substantial number of members of this community to responsible high salaried positions in our government and we further urge the Administration to show equal recognition of the talents possessed by members of our ethnic groups. . . .

The Poles want a share of attention to their economic problems by the federal government. But what they want most is to be accorded a measure of the respect to which their history and their contributions to America entitle them.

3

Varieties of
Ethnic Loyalties
and Affiliations

A common problem facing all major white ethnic groups is the difficulty of identifying the elements and characteristics that keep them together. The degree of difficulty differs from group to group. It is relatively easy to define the "Jewishness" of the Jewish group or the "Polishness" of American Poles, but it is much harder to isolate the "Italianness" of the American Italians or the "Irishness" of the American Irish.

"Jewishness"
"Jewishness" seems relatively clear to Jews, but it does present somewhat of a puzzle to non-Jews. Many find it difficult to understand why Jews cling so stubbornly to their separate existence as a people, even in circumstances where their total assimilation may be possible. The adherence to the Old Testament and the rejection of the New Testament was long thought to be the only reason for the survival of the Jewish people. In more modern times, some Christians find it peculiar that Jews who are not religious,

who declare themselves to be agnostics or atheists, think of themselves and are considered by others as Jews. Novak suggested, with a great deal of insight, that Jews are experts in hiding their deep attachment to their roots in order to survive in alien societies. The reason for this developed trait lies in the long history of the Jews. What unites them is a memory of their long, turbulent, and often glorious past, a recognition of their interdependence in the lands of their dispersion, and shared goals and aspirations for the future, chief among them being the security of the State of Israel. "Jewishness" denotes also a strong belief in the basic goodness of man, in the worth-whileness of life on earth, coupled with a substantial dose of scepticism about an after life, and an unshaken belief in the unlimited opportunities to improve the quality of life for people everywhere. *Tikkun Olam*—the betterment of the world—is an ancient tenet in Jewish mysticism and has been accepted by many Jews as a life's obligation. Hence, the "Jewish heart," "Jewish idealism," and "Jewish liberalism."

The sources of Jewish liberalism extend to the early history of the Jewish people and are the consequences of the long experience of almost 2,000 years of sojourns in the many lands of the Diaspora. Responsibility for the plight of the poor, the widows, and the orphans has been a part of the Jewish religion which stresses *this* worldliness. Since the promise of immortality and of a better life after death play a relatively minor role in Jewish religious thinking, the right of every person to a good life on this earth becomes paramount. The injunction, in Deuteronomy 15, verse 7, reads:

> If there be among you a poor man or one of the brethren within any of the gates in thy land which the Lord God giveth thee, thou shalt not harden thine heart, nor shut thine hand from thy brother.

The Bible and the Talmud contain a series of welfare laws including the cancellation of debts every seventh year, the reversion of the land to the original owners every fifty years, and the setting aside by each landowner of a portion of his land at harvest time for the poor. The needy of Israel have, on the basis of Biblical laws and the teachings of the Prophets, considered it their *right* to be taken care of by their community. Significantly, the word charity in Hebrew, *Tzdakah*, comes from the word *Tzedek*, which means justice. Thus, the giving of charity was and is expected of every Jew, and it became a virtual law for every Jewish community to take care of its poor and destitute. This attitude to charity accounts for the enormous sums of money that American Jews contribute every year for hospitals, Jewish centers, schools, and theological seminaries and for the State of Israel.

The experience of the Jews during the centuries of living in many lands under many different regimes has taught them that there is a direct correlation between extreme right-wing or extreme left-wing, military and reactionary governments and anti-Semitism and repression. Contrariwise, they usually lived in relative security and prospered in countries ruled by progressive, liberal governments. Czarist Russia, with its "Pale of Settlement," the restricted area where Jews were allowed to live, with its rampant anti-Semitism, ritual blood murder trials, and pogroms became a classic example of how an unenlightened, despotic regime treated the Jews within its borders. Periods of relaxation in political repression, succeeded by liberal reforms like that following the 1905 Revolution in Russia always brought an improvement in the lot of the Jews. The communist dictatorship of the Soviet Union proved to be as bad for the Jews as the reactionary regime of Czars.

Jews suffered persecution from the "colonels" regime in pre-war Poland and were later mistreated by the communist governments of Gomulka and Gierik. On the other hand, the French Revolution brought emancipation to the Jews, and English Jews prospered under the benevolent constitutional monarchy in modern England. The long rule of Emperor Franz Joseph of the Austro-Hungarian Empire, a ruler whose power was limited by a government that included Austrians, Poles, and Hungarians, was fondly re-

membered by the large number of Jews who lived in
southern Poland, Czechoslovakia, Slovenia, and Hungary,
all of which were part of the empire. Generally speaking,
dictatorships, military juntas, states that had an established
religion, and governments that were oblivious to the poverty and sufferings of the poor and the underprivileged,
have proven to be bad risks for Jews. The same is and
was the case with the totalitarian states on the left. Those
lessons have not been forgotten by the Jews. Hence their
special devotion to the United States of America and to
liberalism.

The devotion of Jews to the State of Israel has a great
deal to do with the Jewish past, with Jews' appraisal
of their position in the world today, and with their aspirations for the future. The depth of the passionate devotion
of American Jews to Israel is rarely understood by the
gentile world. In essence, Jewish attachment to Palestine
and to Jerusalem, the city of Zion and their former glory,
has never weakened. The Nazi holocaust, which resulted
in the mass murder of 6 million Jews (many of whom
could have been saved if there had been a country ready
to take them), has convinced American Jews that there
must be an independent State of Israel ready and willing
to serve as a haven of refuge for those Jews who wish to
settle there. Furthermore, most American Jews seem to be
convinced, rightly or wrongly, that the destruction of
Israel would be detrimental, if not disastrous, to their
status in the United States. They are proud of the political,
economic, and social progress made by Israel, and especially of the courage and valor of the Israeli army. They
see in the widely praised record of victories of the Israeli
army at least a partial recompense for the humiliation
suffered when they helplessly watched Hitler's minions
slaughter 6 million of their brethren.

While many American Jews have only a vague knowledge of Jewish history and Jewish culture, they know
what their "Jewishness" means to them. If they sometimes
falter in that understanding, there is always the outside
world ready to remind them that they are Jews. Unlike

the Poles, the Italians, and other white ethnics, Jewish ethnicity is not only a matter of choice; it is, in large measure, forced on the Jews by the society at large. Even Jews who become Christian Scientists or Unitarians are still considered Jews by the general society.

"Polishness"

To ethnically minded Poles, "Polishness" means Polish patriotism, a deep devotion to the ideal of a free Poland. It includes a special affection and reverence for the Polish language, which goes beyond the acknowledgement of its usefulness as a language of communication and the language of their literature. Poles love their language, and this is true even for many American Poles who do not speak Polish, because it served them well as an instrument of national survival. Poles still sing with deep emotion these lines contained in a poem by Maria Konopnicka: "We shall not allow our language to be forgotten, we are the Polish nation, the Polish people, a tribe descended from the dynasty of Piast kings . . . we shall not be buried. . . ."

"Polishness" includes a deep reverence for the Catholic Church, or more accurately, for the *Polish* Catholic Church. To a Pole, Polish religious customs are part not only of his Catholic faith but of his Polish nationality. While ethnic groups in America observe some special customs, most of which they brought over from the country of their origin, no ethnic group has made its customs as much a part of its cultural and religious ethos as the American Poles. Holiday customs, particularly, have become important characteristics of Polish culture and the "Polishness" of American Poles. The observances of Polish religious customs have sometimes presented problems for the Polish churches in America, especially the Christmas custom of blessing the *Oplatek*, a thin, unleavened bread of flour and water, which is broken and eaten in a special family ceremony, and the blessing of the Easter food baskets. Irish bishops, who, as a rule, have jurisdiction over Polish parishes, have often considered these Polish religious customs as irrelevant pagan relics and have refused to sanction them. They have also looked with disfavor on sermons delivered in Polish or on the teaching of the Polish language in parochial schools. The Irish church hierarchy had as its goal the establishment of a united Catholic Church in America and considered the demands of the Polish parishioners to be narrow and divisive. "Ours," James Cardinal Gibbons, of Baltimore, said, "is the American Church, not Irish, German, Italian, or Polish, and we keep it American."

Cardinal Gibbons' attitude had a great deal of logic behind it. The heads of the Catholic Church in America, faced with large-scale immigrations of Italian, German, Croatian, French Canadian, and Polish Catholics, considered it imperative to minimize the differences in Catholic religious schools and observances. They were determined to establish a united and an Americanized Catholic Church in the United States. But Polish-American historians and scholars are unsparing in condemning the Irish cardinals and bishops for using their authority to force Polish priests and nuns to de-Polonize their churches.

In *Poles in American History and Tradition,* Professor Joseph Wyrtwal writes,

> But their (the Poles') effort to create autonomous religious institutions where the humblest and the meanest would receive a cordial welcome and a psychic pleasure that was not found in Irish or German Catholic churches, was limited by the American Catholic hierarchy . . . the Irish bishops were determined to deprive the Poles of their language and culture.

Dr. Eugene Kusielewicz goes even further: "The low status of the Polish Americans is directly traceable to the fact that the Poles, unlike the Jews and the Ukrainians were not allowed to control their own churches."

One of the most crucial dilemmas facing the American Polish community and endangering its future is its inability or unwillingness to support academic institutions where Polish language, culture, and scholarship would be at the center of concern. The largest and the most prestigious Polish organization, the Polish National Alliance, which

has over 300,000 members and which is also a wealthy
insurance company, supports one academic institution, the
Alliance College in Cambridge Springs, Pennsylvania. This
liberal arts college, which has an enrollment of about 600
students, about half of them Polish Americans, offers the
usual Bachelor of Arts and Science degrees, but students
may also major in Polish language, Polish arts, and Polish
literature. The college is in an almost constant financial
crisis, and the Alliance has had to increase its subsidies
almost every year. One difficult problem is that the college
has an enrollment substantially lower than its capacity.

The other large Polish organization, the Polish Roman
Catholic Union, with a membership of over 160,000, supports a small theological seminary, where Polish priests
are trained, and Saint Mary's College, a four-year liberal
arts college. Both are located at Orchard Lake, Michigan.
The total enrollment of both colleges is around 200. Recently, the institution has expanded to include a Polish
Culture Center, which has published some scholarly mono-
graphs and textbooks.

These efforts are commendable, but they cannot com-
pare with the Notre Dames and the Fordhams of the Irish
or with the Jewish Theological Seminary, Brandeis University, Dropsie College, and the Hebrew Union College
maintained by the Jews. The budget of many of these institutions, taken separately, exceed the total budget of all
Polish academic institutions. Somehow, Polish leaders have
as yet been unable to initiate a program of vast cultural
activities for youth and adults that would decisively en-
hance the image of the American Poles. In addition, these
institutions would provide an opportunity for many Polish
scholars in America to pursue their studies in relative
security and in the public eye.

The Italian-Americans
How do Italians perceive their own ethnic entity?
"Italianness" is not only a strange and unwieldy term in
comparison to "Jewishness" and "Polishness," but it is also

a concept which is difficult to define in terms of the life of the Italian-American community in America. What does being an Italian mean to an Italian-American? It certainly does not mean the same kind of fierce nationalist devotion to Italy as the Poles have to a free Poland or that the Jews have to a sovereign and secure Israel. At least, this impression is left from the reading of the Italian-American press (both in Italian and in English) and from the pronouncements issued by the leading Italian-American organizations. Of course, it can be argued that Italy is free, sovereign, and secure under the NATO treaty, and Italian-Americans have no cause to be jittery about its future. Nevertheless, while love for Italy and justified pride in Italian culture, art, and literature are evident and increasing among the American-Italians, fierce Italian nationalism seems to be alien to their nature. In that they are not unlike their compatriots in Italy, who, while caught for a brief period in a chauvinistic frenzy of Mussolini, soon tired of this aberration. The stress in the cultural work of the Italian-American organizations is on the study of Italian language, art, and music.

A reporter for the *New York Times* wrote that Italians of many walks of life, of the first, second, and third generation, vary greatly in the degree of their identification with the Italian community. "The Italians in New York," the reporter, Richard Severo, wrote, "do not agree about who they are, what progress they have made, since the great migrations of half a century ago, and where they should be going. And yet this people, whose identity is so difficult to define, has recently been thrust very much into the public eye." Severo recalled the mass picketing and demonstrations of New York Italians to protest the use of the word Mafia by the F.B.I. and the communications media and the strong showing of Italians who abandoned their usually Democratic voting pattern to support Governor Nelson Rockefeller and to elect the conservative James Buckley to the U.S. Senate for New York. In spite of this evidence of ethnic cohesion, Severo quoted Dr. John A. B. Faggi, director of Columbia University's Casa Italiana:

They [the Italian Americans] are not a closely knit group in any sense . . . they take [pride] in being part of the great Romano-Italian civilization. . . . But mostly they share an overriding sense of responsibility as American citizens and that, they are, not Italian.

The poet, John Ciardi, whose parents were immigrants, predicted that "within another ten years, you won't even be able to classify the Italians as an ethnic group."

On the other hand, many Italian organizations claim a rapid growth in membership—the Americans of Italian Descent, based in New York, for example, and many of the organizations comprising the Joint Civic Committee of Italian-Americans in Chicago and similar organizations in other cities. Professor Luciano J. Iorizza, a distinguished American-Italian historian, commented on Severo's article in a letter to the *New York Times* (November 23, 1972, p. 17). He said that a growing number of scholars of Italian descent in America are devoting their talents to an intensive study of the Italian community. More importantly, Professor Iorizza noted that an "ever increasing number of Italian-American college students are becoming inquisitive about their immigrant parents . . . beneath the exterior, fierce individualism generally posed by Italo-Americans is a sense of group consciousness recognized and nurtured by some leaders of the Italian masses."

Probably the most reliable assessment of the state of ethnic awareness of Italian-Americans comes from a distinguished scholar and author, Father Silvano Tomasi, director of the Center for Migration Studies on Staten Island. Tomasi's studies have led him to conclude that the Italian-American community in America divides into three groups, the "Italian Italians," who are the recent immigrants who speak Italian almost exclusively, then come the Italian-Americans of Mulberry Street in New York and of the "Little Italies" in many big cities who have been in this country for many years and whose feelings of ethnic identity are strong and who are active in the Italian-American organizations. Finally, there is the third group comprised of second and third generation Americans of

Italian descent, many of whom are college educated businessmen and professionals. "This group," Father Tomasi said, "are still proud of their heritage, perhaps, but [they] do not identify with Italian-American problems or organizations. They do not participate. Their ethnic awareness is limited to their food, to the arts, to the Italian-made movies and sometimes to their history."

Father Paul J. Asciolla, editor of *Fra Noi* admitted that,

> no one really knows how many Italian-Americans—who identify themselves as such—there are in the Chicago metro area. . . . Seeing the same faces at meetings and banquets after a long period of time causes many to wonder . . . *there is no one huge monolithic, determined Italian-American community, united on common goals for the future.* . . . We have to face the fact that some people do not identify with being Italian-American and they could care less. . . . There is still however a sizeable number of people who are true believers that are good Americans with an appreciation of their Italian and/or Italian-American Heritage. . . .

What Father Asciolla has said here about the Italian-Americans is largely true of Polish-Americans, Jewish-Americans, Greek-Americans, and many other white ethnic minorities. This realistic appraisal of the size and the level of ethnic identity puts a special obligation on the spokesmen of the ethnic groups to be much more careful and, yes, more modest about their claims and demands both *vis-à-vis* in their own communities and in reference to the general community.

As yet, the increased interest in ethnic identity has not translated itself into financial support for Italian-American cultural youth centers or American-Italian institutions of higher learning. In fact, Italian-Americans do not maintain any institutions of higher learning in the United States. It seems that they are still adhering to the long tradition of southern Italians and look with suspicion on civic activities as aimed to benefit and enrich some greedy individuals. However, in recent years, some progress can be noted. A few courageous Italian priests have built an

Italian cultural center on the edge of Chinatown in Los Angeles, and the Chicago Italians maintain a splendid home for the Italian aged, the Villa Scalabroni. Generally, however, American-Italians have yet to make adequate provisions for cultural activities in their community.

The Italian-American community still struggles with an old problem—how to dissociate itself from the tiny minority of Italians who are prominent leaders of organized crime in America. For many years, nativists and assorted xenophobes perpetuated the myth that Italian immigrants had an innate "criminal instinct," which drove them to criminal activities. No scientific evidence has ever been offered to support these assertions. For years, following the large-scale Irish immigration, newspapers wrote about the Irish propensity for crime. Hollywood produced many movies with actors speaking with an Irish brogue, who played Irish-American gangsters. Today, with the same reckless disregard for scientific evidence, many racists are convinced that blacks are "natural" killers, muggers, and rapists.

Many Italian-American scholars and journalists have also pointed out that crime was never an Italian monopoly. That, of course, is true. In Chicago, in the lawless 1920s, there operated, in addition to the Colossimo, Torio, and Capone gangs, the all Irish gangs of the O'Donnell brothers, the powerful O'Banion gang, and the Polish gang of Joe Saltis. But in the course of years, the Irish prospered and abandoned the rackets. They, in fact, became the cops who were fighting crime activities. Polish immigrants never became attracted to crime activities to any appreciable extent. The Polish Catholic Church was too effective to allow such straying from law and order. For a variety of reasons, Italians, almost all of Sicilian descent, remained prominent in organized crime in the big cities across the country. While at most, the number of Italian-Americans in the crime gangs is less than 6,000, these criminals taint the image of millions of hard working and law abiding Italian-Americans. A deep sense of unease and insecurity sweeps the Italian community in America, when

a Senate Committee or another national investigative body
holds hearings on organized crime and the suspected heads
of crime activities virtually all bearing Italian names are
forced by subpoenas to testify, or at least to appear. The
same is true of newspaper stories, reporting the continuous
murderous wars among some of the crime "families." It
matters little to the general reading public whether Italian-
American historians and sociologists are right or wrong
when they present evidence to prove that the existence of
the Mafia as a nationwide criminal conspiracy is a myth.
Impressive evidence for this conclusion was recently presented by Professor Francis Ianni of Columbia University.
The general reader may agree, but he considers it irrelevant whether or not the various crime organizations in New
York, Boston, and Chicago communicate and cooperate
with each other. What is significant to him—and this as-
pect presents a serious question for the image of the
American-Italians—is the fact that revelations about organized crime consistently mention Italian names.

Accepting the point of view of several Italian-American
scholars that a nationwide crime organization does not
exist, a number of Italian-American organizations pressured the federal government to ban the use of the word
"Mafia" from official releases. In July, 1970, Attorney
General John Mitchell complied and sent a memorandum
to law enforcement agencies banning the use of the words
"Mafia" and "Cosa Nostra" because, as he put it, these
terms offended the feelings of "decent Italian-Americans."
The effect of this ban, predictably, has been negligible,
because most of the newspapers and radio and television
stations continue to refer to "Mafia figures," "Mafiosi,"
etc.

The problem of how to dissociate the overwhelming
majority of law-abiding Italian-Americans from the small
minority of criminals is still plaguing the Italian-American
community. Americans must, as Father Asciolla wrote in
the *Chicago Tribune*, stop making the terms "Mafia" and
"organized crime" synonymous and interchangeable with
the words "Italian-American." Equally troublesome is the

dilemma of third-generation Italian-Americans, who, for a variety of reasons, wish to keep or return to their ethnic roots to define the meanings of their "Italianness." Professor Richard Gambino, writing in the *New York Times*, makes some interesting observations on the alternatives that are facing young Italian-Americans:

> They may opt for one of the several models that have served other ethnic groups. For example, they may choose to cultivate their Italian culture, pursue personal careers, and fuse the two into an energetic and confident relationship—which has been characteristic of the Jewish-Americans. They may also turn toward the church, revive and build upon its power base a political organization and morale, as Irish-American did. Or, they may feel it necessary to form strictly nationalistic power blocs as some black Americans are doing.

A few observations on these alternatives may highlight the complexity in dealing with white ethnic groups. There is little evidence to support Gambino's assertion that young Jews have successfully fused Jewish culture with their careers in the general society. In fact, evidence seems to indicate that in spite of the millions of dollars invested by American Jews in religious and cultural schools and universities, many young American Jews have become alienated from their culture and have found that the fusion between their Jewish roots and the American environment is quite difficult to achieve.

American Jews and the White Ethnic Strategy

The newspaper columnist Dorothy Thomson once said that the "Jews are like other people—only more so." What she probably meant was that Jews face, as a group, the same or similar problems as other groups, except that in the case of the Jews, the issues and the dilemmas are, or seem to be not amenable to a simple definition, and solutions seem to be more difficult. This is the case when attempts are made to analyze the status and the future of the 5 or 5.5 million American Jews.

On the surface, the status of American Jews seems to be very secure. Jews are the most affluent of all the white ethnic groups. With the exception of small pockets of poverty, mainly in some sections of Brooklyn and the Bronx, Jews live in well-to-do sections of the big cities and in many upper-middle-class suburbs. In 1972, Professor Marvin V. Verbit, of Brooklyn College, conducted a study of the 25,000 Jews in North Jersey, which is typical of findings in Jewish communities in other big cities. The findings were based on demographic data gathered from 1,722 households and interviews with 631 individuals.

The study disclosed that there are more professionals (doctors, lawyers, dentists, educators) in the Jewish Federation of the North Jersey area than in any other single occupational category, and that about two-thirds of the working Jews are salaried and one-third are self-employed. Twenty percent are owners or managers of businesses. Less than 4 percent of all employed Jews are unskilled laborers. College attendance of the young is almost universal. This demographic data would not be much different in the Jewish suburbs of Chicago, Philadelphia, Boston, New York, or San Francisco.

It may be cautiously postulated that the general affluence of the Jewish community is at the root of many of the problems and difficulties afflicting the American Jewish community. Paradoxically, this general affluence has been the main cause of the loss of political influence of the Jews in both major parties. In Chicago, for instance, Jews who were concentrated in a number of areas like the 24th Ward on the West Side have moved *en masse* to the suburbs, where their political power has been diffused, especially in local and state elections. The time when Jewish political leaders like Colonel Jacob Arvey were able to deliver a solid Jewish vote in a number of wards to the Democratic city and county machine is long over. Consequently, Mayor Daley does not consider Jews a reliable source of votes, and that has been reflected in fewer and fewer Jews being slated for important political jobs in the city, Cook County, and the state. Only the relatively unimportant positions of City Treasurer and Sheriff are held by Jews; the real political power is shared by Irish-Americans, Polish-Americans, blacks, and Italians.

A similar situation prevails on the national scale. Jews have lost influence in the Democratic Party, where they wielded a great deal of power in the days of F.D.R.'s New Deal and during the presidencies of Harry Truman and John F. Kennedy. They were an important part of the Grand Democratic Coalition, which included some Protestants, many Catholics, blacks, labor unions, and various white ethnic minority groups. In this coalition, liberal Jews had political power because they were concentrated in large cities and because they cast their votes in large numbers for Democratic candidates. Now, as in Chicago, many Jews have moved to the suburbs, where their political power is insignificant as contrasted with the usually large Republican vote usually recorded in wealthy suburbs.

As we have seen, this new political reality and the strained relations between the white ethnic groups and the blacks in the big cities have caused influential Jewish organizations, like the American Jewish Committee, to develop the so-called "ethnic strategy." This strategy calls for the initiation of a series of dialogues, and if possible, of an alliance with the larger white ethnic groups to form a new coalition that would eventually develop a more meaningful relationship with the black community. This new cooperation with the Poles, the Italians, and other white ethnics who often find themselves in bitter competition with blacks in the areas of housing and school busing has of necessity brought a weakening, or at least a muting, of the long standing commitment of the major Jewish organizations to the cause of civil rights. Consequently, Jewish-black relations are experiencing a period of strain. The report of a task force commissioned by the American Jewish Committee, headed by Morris Abrams as chairman and Professor Seymour Martin Lipset of Harvard as consultant, states that the rising extremism and militancy of the blacks has brought about a feeling of solidarity in defense of their neighborhoods and good schools of the white ethnic groups. The report continues,

In their quest for solutions of these problems and for the defense of the rights of groups other than blacks, the Jews, the proto-ethnic group, also rediscovered ethnicity. Jewish leadership's awareness of these changes, and the need to find coalition allies among the diverse groups in dealing with the situation is reflected in the work of the National Project on Ethnic America.

The report of the task force, *Group Life in America,* put the issue succinctly:

American Jewry has been heavily liberal in its ideology and organizational strategies. And organized liberalism has cooperated closely with Jewry on issues of Jewish rights, anti-Semitism, assistance to the State of Israel, and support for rights of other deprived minorities. The change in liberal foreign policy affects Israel. The dismay over the inefficacy of applying traditional universalistic and in-tegrationist principles to the condition of the blacks challenges norms and institutions which Jews have long regarded essential to their own security. And the Jews, confused by the same sense of inadequacy which upsets the liberals, are at crossroads. *They are* divided on what is to be done, as they have not been since the rise of Nazism.

The dilemma of disillusionment with liberalism and the move to a more conservative stance is well stated by the task force. The question whether the "white ethnic strategy" pursued by the Jewish leaders is the right strategy is at least open to question. This strategy calls for the Jews to be the mediators, the convenors, the middlemen between the white ethnics and the blacks. To learn from the lessons of long Jewish history, Jews have never fared well as middlemen or conciliators between antagonistic and warring sections of the population. Time and again, both sides would turn on the mediators and make them the convenient scapegoats for their frustrations. Furthermore, it is an illusion, as we shall see, to look upon the white ethnic groups as a united body of population. In truth while the Poles, Lithuanians, the Italians, the Ukrainians, and the Serbs and the Croats and others are united in their grievances against the blacks, and against the general society (most of these grievances are not shared by Jews), their mutual distrust, old feuds, and even hatreds among themselves are quite evident. It is, for instance, questionable whether American Serbs fear and distrust Negroes more than they fear and distrust American Croats or that Poles could indeed cooperate on common problems with the Lithuanians.

There is evidence to suggest that while Jews, especially their intellectual elite, have been jolted in their liberalism, primarily by the militancy of the blacks, by a danger to the merit systems for advancement and promotion, in the big-city school systems and universities and by the specter of the quota system. However, American Jews seem to be clinging to their traditional liberalism.

The Harris Poll results published on October 12, 1972, in the *New York Times* centered on the political attitudes of the Jews and the Italian-Americans. The results revealed that while Italian-Americans have moved considerably to the right, Jews have retained their adherence to liberal positions.

Predictions about the success of the American Jewish community in grappling with its dilemmas are virtually impossible. All that one can say is that we are dealing here with an old people, which has often proved its prophets of doom to be false prophets.

4

Jane Addams, Hull House, and the Education of the Immigrants

Probably the best laboratory for the study of the process of adjustment, acculturation, or assimilation of the immigrants and their children was the Hull House settlement houses in Chicago. And the most competent observer of this process was Jane Addams, who founded Hull House in 1889 at the time when the tidal waves of immigration from Europe to America were already changing the composition of the American society.

Hull House served the immigrants—parents, adults, and children—as an adult recreation and education center. In the broader sense, it was a school or a series of schools for the young. The influence of Jane Addams on public schooling, both by the example of the programs offered at Hull House and through her own efforts, was great and pervasive. Since that phase of Jane Addams' life has been somewhat neglected, it is important to see how her views and activities contributed to the new conceptions of the role of the public schools and education in a society so changed by the great influx of immigrants.

The bibliography on the life and work of Jane Addams is varied and extensive. Several biographies were written by writers and historians, and her own works have been republished many times and are still read widely. One question that seems to have fascinated many writers concerns an analysis of the motives that caused her to dedicate her long life to Hull House. The question is important and interesting, but the historians' preoccupation with this issue seems to have distracted them from a detailed examination of Jane Addams' educational philosophy and record in the education of the immigrants and their children. In this generally neglected area in the history of American education, the thoughts and work of the founder of Hull House deserve a great deal of space and attention.

Those who have paid some attention to her contributions seem to have experienced some special difficulty in dealing with the subject. They apparently found it difficult to believe that a rich, WASP, young lady from an upper-middle-class family, the daughter of a banker, a mill owner, and a state senator could have learned to understand the plight of large numbers of immigrants in the painful process of their adjustment to the American society. The education of Jane Addams was typical of a well-born young American lady. It culminated in graduation from the Rockford Seminary for Women, which proudly called itself the "Mount Holyoke of the West." The curriculum in the seminary included the study of Greek, English literature, moral philosophy, history, some science, and a great deal of religious training aimed at preparing many of the ladies to become Christian missionaries.

The home background and the education of Jane Addams caused some writers to suggest that she turned to settlement work in the grimy Chicago neighborhood of Polk and Halstead streets because she became bored with the life and the activities of her social milieu. One recent biographer wrote that after her graduation from college and after the customary grand tour of Europe, "she did not have a goal or an occupation, or any thing useful to do." This undoubtedly is a true assessment of her predicament just prior to the opening of Hull House in 1889. It may well be that in the early period of her settlement work, Hull House was for Jane Addams merely a philanthropic endeavor. But, in a relatively short period of time, it became a cause to which she happily decided to devote her entire life even to the exclusion of her personal interests.

Why and how did this change take place? It came, primarily, because she learned a great deal about the lives of the many thousands of Italians, Greeks, Jews, Irish, and Bohemians who flocked to the many activities of Hull House and concluded that she could and wanted to be of assistance to them in the realization of their hopes and aspirations. Jane Addams developed a well-thought-out philosophy about the best way to help the large waves of immigrants and their children to adjust to the new and strange American environment. This philosophy was far more perceptive than the simple and often xenophobic notions of "Americanization" which were widely entertained by many of her prominent contemporaries. In the spirit of the time this was no small achievement.

Some writers have failed to perceive the substantial difference between the views on immigration and the immigrants of Jane Addams and those of the other leaders of the Reform and Progressive Movement. For instance she supported and admired Theodore Roosevelt, a leading Progressive, but she vigorously opposed his extreme views on the Americanization of the immigrants. She also does not fit very well in the general interpretation of the motives of the Progressive leaders who in the view of one of the most brilliant historians of the period, Richard Hofstadter, were members of the socially alienated groups who turned to reform out of a sense of guilt because they lived in comparative luxury in the midst of the squalor of the cities.

It seemed natural to put Jane Addams in that group. She was alienated from her social milieu, and she was rich and bored. Christopher Lasch correctly pointed out that at the time of the founding of the Hull House she did not feel guilty about the sorry lot of the workers and the poor who were victims of industrialism. In Lasch's view, at that period of her life, she was rebelling against her family, and especially against her mother, who wanted her to lead a life of leisure as befitted her station in life. She did not feel, Lasch added, that she was making a sacrifice by helping the poor and the immigrants, and she did not have a condescending attitude toward them. She was dedicated to "bridging the chasm that industrialism has opened between social classes." But the American people made Jane Addams a saint, Lasch concluded, and she became a national myth—and the myth of Jane Addams served to render her harmless as a social critic.

In the *New Radicalism in America,* Lasch is even more skeptical about her effectiveness as a social worker and reformer. "The trouble was that Jane Addams was asking, in effect, that young people be adjusted to a social order which by her own admission was cynically indifferent to their welfare." The American industrial society was in her eyes guilty of oppressing and repressing the workers who served it, but according to Lasch she made no attempt to change the system. Her only aim was to make it function more smoothly. In fact, Lasch maintains, the educational efforts of the head of Hull House were aimed at fostering the ideal of "social control" so well articulated by her friend John Dewey.

Lasch's critique apparently was too mild for a member of the group of younger revisionist historians of American education, Paul Violas, who sees Jane Addams' view of the immigrants as paternalistic and her reforms not as liberal or enlightened but conservative, or even reactionary. Her entire life's work was dedicated, says Violas, to "an attempt to replace the social control implicit in the village community in the countries of origin of the immigrant Italians, Greeks and others with the controls more suitable to an urban environment." Violas charges that Jane Addams' "system of beliefs was based not on dedication to individual freedom but on an advocacy of an organic society acting as a collective association."

Somehow, in Violas' view, these two commitments are mutually exclusive. Ignoring a great deal of what Jane Addams had written and done to combat the feeling of alienation and boredom on the part of individual workers, Violas insists that she saw individualism as a plague in the American urbanized and industrialized society. This, he says, was a repressive philosophy aimed at keeping the workers from demanding material changes and improvements in the American society.

Quoting single words like "primitive," "illiterate," "clannish," "single," and others, all taken, without any indication of their context or reference, from her many books and essays, Violas concludes that she had contempt for the immigrants. "The immigrant, for Jane Addams, presented a threat," Violas writes, "because his different ethnic background disrupted American cultural unity. The relative ease, however, with which he could be stripped of his cultural foundations and reduced to the simplest elements of humanity enhanced his value as a building block for her new community." Violas also charges her with using Hull House to engage in a propaganda scheme, employing effective devices of mass psychology with the purpose of defusing social conflicts. "Throughout her discussions of the recreational activities at Hull House," Violas writes, "one finds rationale for social control through the manipulation of subconscious and non-rational impulses."

Michael Katz, a more careful revisionist historian of American education, in a thoughtful review of *Roots of Crisis* in *Harvard Educational Review* took issue with Violas' contention. "Violas also suggests," Katz stated, "that her insistence on the importance of popularizing ideas indicates she believed in the legitimacy and necessity of propaganda. But his quotations from her writings do not show anything of the sort."

Katz objects to the absence of evidence to support
Violas' contention about Jane Addams' views on manipulation of public opinion. His objection applies equally to
Violas' conclusions about her views on the immigrants and
on the education of their children. Charitably, one can say
that Violas read the books and articles of Jane Addams
rather hastily, looking only for confirmation of his pre-
conceived ideas. His is not a serious or correct analysis of
her attitude to the immigrants or of her philosophy about
the acculturation of the immigrants. It also seems that
Violas knows little about the educational and recreational
activities in Hull House.

While Christopher Lasch's essays on Jane Addams are
perceptive and innovative, his conclusion that Jane
Addams was a supporter of the social status quo is, in
the light of her record and writings, off the mark. The
Mayor of Chicago, the political bosses of the city, indus-
trialists like George Pullman would have been astonished
to read that the head of Hull House was a "harmless
social critic." Among other things, the Mayor would have
related the trouble Jane Addams caused him on the issue
of garbage collection on the West Side of Chicago and
how the garbage was collected after she was appointed
Garbage Commissioner of her ward. In the Chicago of
those days, this was no small achievement.

At the time of the founding of Hull House, America
was already a nation of immigrants. Newcomers from
southern and eastern Europe were pouring into the country, often at a rate of 40,000 per day. The 1890 Census
disclosed that 20 million Americans were either foreign
by birth or parentage, while 34 million were classed as
native white Americans. James Bryce expressed the ap-
prehension of many leading Americans when he wrote in
1888 in *The American Commonwealth,*

> Within the last decade new swarms of European immi-
> grants have invaded America, drawn from their homes in
> the eastern part of Central Europe. There seems to be a
> danger that if they continue to come in large number
> they may retain their low standards of decency and com-

fort, and menace the continuance among the working class generally of that far higher standard which has hitherto prevailed in all but a few spots in the country.

Josiah Strong echoed Bryce's sentiments and wrote in *The Twentieth Century City* that while America was indebted to the immigrants "for developing its resources we cannot shut our eyes to the fact that the foreign population, as a whole, is depressing our average in intelligence and morality in the direction of the deadline of crime and ignorance."

Leaders in American society, writers, editors and thinkers, and many influential members of Congress shared the convictions of Bryce and Strong that the immigrants had lower morals, were less intelligent by far than the native Americans, and had a predisposition to crime and to living in unsanitary conditions. Thus it was feared, they could adversely influence, if not contaminate, the superior native American population.

Jane Addams rejected these ideas about the immigrants. Unlike Bryce, Cubberley, Strong, and others, she had direct contact with the immigrants from eastern and southern Europe. In fact, she lived among them and with them and soon developed an affection and respect for them. In *Twenty Years of Hull House,* she described the area around Hull House.

> Between Halstead Street and the river lived about ten thousand Italians—Neapolitans, Sicilians, and Calabrians, with an occasional Lombard and Venetian. To the South on Twelfth Street are many Germans, and side streets are given almost entirely to Polish and Russian Jews. Still farther south, these Jewish colonies merge into a huge Bohemian colony, so vast that Chicago ranks as the third Bohemian city in the world. To the northwest are many Canadian-French, clannish in spite of their long residence in America, and to the north are Irish and first generation of Americans.

Jane Addams made great efforts to learn as much as she could about the various groups of the immigrants. She met them daily in the classrooms, in the cafeteria, and in the many meeting halls in the Hull House buildings. She was an able and a thorough student, and in a relatively short period of time she came to a number of conclusions about her clients. She firmly rejected the attitudes of superiority and contempt toward the immigrants. Her heart overflowed with sympathy for the hardships and the sufferings of the newcomers, mostly peasants, who were suddenly and often savagely exposed to the ruthlessness of the American industrial system. She deplored the working conditions in the sweatshops, the lack of minimum safety precautions, and the rampant exploitation in the huge textile factory of Hart Schaffner and Marx, which was located on Chicago's West Side. Jane Addams was particularly appalled by the practice of "outside piece work," an arrangement by which contractors let families work at home on the cutting and sewing of pants, suits, and dresses and paid them by the number of finished garments. To eke out a meager living, some families, including small children, often worked sixteen hours per day.

But the founder of Hull House did not intend merely to stand by and wring her hands at the sorry lot of the immigrants. She developed a two-fold program of action to combat the exploitation and the deplorable conditions she witnessed. First came the opening of Hull House to various groups in which heated debates about the grievances and the rights of workers were discussed. One such club, "The Working Peoples' Social Science Club" was often attacked by leading businessmen, including supporters of Hull House, as promoting radical ideas. Jane Addams responded by declaring that her settlement house maintained an open door policy to all ideas. "I did not intend," she said, "to be subsidized by millionaires and neither did I propose to be bullied by working men." When the Pullman strike came, Jane Addams was critical of the division of the Chicago community along class lines. In a paper she published on the strike entitled "The Modern King Lear," she maintained that George Pullman bore the major blame for the strike because he expected the gratitude of the workers in exchange for his paternalistic effort to organize their lives in the Pullman community. Pullman, she wrote, gave the workers "sanitary houses and beautiful parks but made no effort to find out their desires, and without any organization through which to give them social expansion." He wanted his workers to live in decency and thrift, Jane Addams wrote, but he deprived them of their right to order their own lives.

Another major effort was directed to alleviating the exploitation of the immigrants. She was successful in influencing the state legislature to pass the first factory law in Illinois, which provided for sanitary conditions in the sweatshops and set the minimum age for the employment of children at 14. Disagreeing with the advocates of "Americanization," Jane Addams repeatedly protested the hostility that so many native Americans exhibited toward the immigrants. Recognizing that the immigrants had a rich cultural heritage and religious and literary values that were worth preserving, she was opposed to the pressure exerted by the public schools and the dominant society on the children of the immigrants to repudiate the culture of their parents. "We were often distressed," she recalled, "by the children of immigrant parents who were ashamed of the pit whence they were digged, who repudiated the language and the customs of their elders, and considered themselves successful as they were able to ignore the past." Unlike the leaders of the nativist, xenophobic movement, Jane Addams wanted the Poles, the Italians, the Bohemians, and other ethnic minorities, to preserve their cultural mores while adjusting to the new life in America. Assimilation for the Italians and Bohemians, Jane Addams observed, often meant disdain for their cultures and the worship of American materialism. To encourage respect for the native cultures of immigrants, the management of Hull House frequently arranged for handicraft and art exhibits and dance and musical festivals in which each immigrant group participated. To the delight of the Italians, Hull House regularly arranged for mass meetings in honor of Garibaldi and Mazzini. Greeks had their Hellenic meetings and festivals and Jewish intellectuals debated Jewish history, Zionism, and Socialism.

Jane Addams, as we mentioned, insisted that her staff members work directly in the homes of the immigrants, often doing menial chores but primarily learning their values, customs, and mode of life. She hoped that the outcome would be mutual respect. "The number of people," she wrote "thus informed is constantly increasing in our American cities, and they may in time remove the reproach of social neglect and indifference which has so long rested upon the citizens of the new world."

Addams did not want to "Anglo-Saxonize" or Americanize the immigrants. On the contrary, long before sociologists like Horace Kallen coined the phrase, she embraced "cultural pluralism" as the desired basic concept pertaining to the American society. In this, as in many other of her ideas on social issues and education, she was far ahead of her time. Her insight into the need to acculturate but not to assimilate the immigrants was remarkable. There were many classes at Hull House where immigrants were taught English to prepare them to take the required examination on the U.S. Constitution in order to become citizens. There were also many courses on United States history and government. These courses and lectures were designed to help the immigrants to understand and to adjust to their new country, but, at the same time, better to understand and appreciate their own cultures. But they were not the usual "Americanization" classes. She observed,

> The aim of all the classes was not to set the immigrants apart from their groups as "Americans". . . . On the contrary the aim was to connect him (the immigrant) with all sorts of people by his ability to understand them as well as by his power to supplement their present surrounding with historic background. . . . In these classes the immigrants have struggled to express in their newly acquired tongue some of those hopes and longings which had so much to do with their immigration.

Violas and other revisionist historians of education who have suggested that Jane Addams shared in the general hostility toward the immigrants and have charged that she manipulated them in order to defuse social conflicts, would do well to go back and examine, with greater care, what she actually did and wrote in the several decades of her Hull House activity.

Far from being a tool of the abrasive and agressive business establishment of Chicago on whose financial support she depended, Jane Addams came to the defense of the rights of the immigrant workers by founding the Immigrant Protective League. When business owners began to harass peddlers by having vagrant youths attack them, Jane Addams organized several ethnic Peddlers Associations to impress upon the city and the police that they had the obligation to protect the Jewish, Italian, and Greek peddlers. She insisted, in spite of a barrage of attacks from the press and the business community, that Hull House practice freedom of speech and freedom of assembly. The 10,000 people who each week availed themselves of the clubroom, the Labor Museum, school rooms, Women's Club buildings, boys' club buildings, gymnasium, the music school, and the lecture halls, heard conservative speakers, liberal university professors, radical union organizers, representatives of business and manufacturing interests, Socialists, Bundists, Zionists, Italian and Czech nationalists, and occasionally even advocates of nonviolent anarchism. Answering the critics who charged that she was turning her settlement into a hotbed of radicalism, Jane Addams replied that she hoped that the demonstration of how Hull House practiced the American ideals of freedom would increase the confidence of the immigrants in American institutions and government. Her credo was simple, as she expressed it in *Twenty Years of Hull House:*

> The Settlement recognizes the need of cooperation, both with the radical and the conservative and from the very nature of the case, the Settlement cannot limit its friends to any political party or economic school.

To question the patriotism of the immigrants, to accuse them of "double loyalty," of harboring subversives and anarchists was a fashionable thing to do in the period of great immigration. These accusations came from the press, the Congress, local, state, and federal law enforcement officials, and from most of the patriotic organizations. Jane Addams never joined this super-patriotic xenophobic hysteria. Instead, courageously and at great personal sacrifice, she stated on many occasions that her direct experience with the many thousands of immigrants convinced her that the immigrants, with few exceptions, "adored America." She called for restraint and fairness by the police, the courts, and the public in dealing with suspected anarchists.

Jane Addams faced the greatest challenge on this issue during the period of the "Red Scare" in the 1920s, following the success of the Bolshevik Revolution. Under attack by the press, the D.A.R., and the American Legion for not being "100% American," because of her advocacy of pacificism and internationalism, she repeatedly condemned the wholesale arrests of leaders of various radical immigrant groups and associations and the suppression of hundreds of foreign language periodicals on unproved charges of subversion. She regretted the "spirit of intolerance which had spread over our time choking free sensibilities" and expressed concern that these excesses would further alienate the immigrants from American society. "There is no doubt," she wrote in the second volume of her autobiography, "that the immigrant population in the United States suffered from a sense of ostracism after the war, which in spite of many difficulties, sorrows and despairs, they had never before encountered, in such a universal fashion." In the face of the overwhelming cry in the press and in Congress to limit immigration for central and southern Europe, she opposed the "quota laws." She truly believed in the theory that constituted an amalgamation of the concepts of the melting pot and cultural pluralism and was convinced that American democracy was not endangered by the tremendous influx of non-Nordic immigrants. On the contrary, she firmly believed that America would emerge richer and stronger because of the infusion of the skills and talents brought by newcomers and because of its ability to make use of the contributions of the various immigrant groups.

She spoke and wrote in defense of the immigrants and maintained that if some immigrants had a feeling of hostility to America, it was a response to the animosity they encountered and to the brazen attempts of some Americanizers to deprecate their heritage. "Is the Universe friendly?" said Jane Addams, "is a question that people ask, but this question never presses so hard upon the bewildered human creature as it does upon a stranger in a strange land when his very mother tongue, his inherited customs and mores, his clothing, his food, are all subjected to ridicule and considered per se un-American, if not indeed dangerous and subversive of American institutions."

Slowly the feeling of sympathy for the immigrants became mingled in Jane Addams' mind with a sense of appreciation for their ability to rise rapidly in a basically hostile environment. She noted the many young Jews, Bohemians, and Greeks did well in colleges and became doctors, lawyers, and successful businessmen. Jane Addams was an outspoken supporter and admirer of Sidney Hillman, the leader of the Amalgamated Clothing Workers of America, who in 1915 settled a strike in the largest clothing factory in Chicago by a pact which provided for a high degree of cooperation between the employers and the employees. Hillman stated publicly that the union was interested in the company making good profits because the workers would benefit from its prosperity. Jane Addams, to whom the ideal of industrial and social peace was very dear, commented: "perhaps this great industrial experiment in Chicago founded upon an agreement between the workers and the employers, was easier to bring about among immigrants than it would have been among native born."

Jane Addams developed a comprehensive philosophy of education with particular reference to the role of the public schools in the education of the children of the immigrants. She had need for such a philosophy because Hull House was a huge educational institution serving thousands of adults, teenagers, and children in clubs and formal classes. Throughout her life, Jane Addams was interested in public education, and in 1905 she became a member of the Chicago Board of Education.

She set down her views on education and on schooling in her largely overlooked book, *Democracy and Social Ethics,* which came out in 1902, eight years before the publication of her famous autobiography. In her philosophy of education, Jane Addams was influenced by her friend and co-worker John Dewey, but much of her educational thinking was original. Unlike Dewey, who hardly recognized the problem and the complexity of educating the hundreds of thousands of children of immigrants, Miss Addams was keenly aware of this complex dilemma. In her views on democracy, Jane Addams shared the pragmatic outlook of Dewey and of her other dear friend, Henry James. She believed that the real test of a successful democracy is not its profession of a creed of the freedom, dignity, and equality of men but the extent to which it allows all its citizens to live in freedom, dignity, and equality. American society must be educated to the ideal of "industrial amelioration," or a peaceful co-existence of the workers and the owners of industry. Such an amelioration can only come by a spirit of cooperation among the workers, industry, society, and the government.

Accepting Dewey's position, Jane Addams postulated that the aim of schooling was to free the innate powers and abilities of each child and "connect him" with the rest of life. The pupil must be helped to see his productive place in the society. She was impatient with purely cognitive objectives of school curricula. "We are impatient," she wrote, "with the schools which lay all stress on reading and writing, suspecting them to rest upon the assumption that the ordinary experience of life is worth little and that all knowledge and interest must be brought to the children through the medium of books." Citing the example of the Italian colony in the Hull House neighborhood, Jane Addams observed that Italian parents take their children, especially boys, out of school at the age of thirteen or fourteen, and that these children, exposed to "bookish" education, were not prepared for the harsh reality of life as factory workers or apprentices. She noted that for these Italian children, the family and the street constituted a far greater influence than did the public schools. They learned at home and on the street the skills and values that they needed to *survive* in a hostile society. Italian children had little motivation for learning, and they often shared their parents' doubts whether schooling was a road to economic success. They knew that many of those in their community who became affluent had hardly any education.

To remedy this situation, Jane Addams demanded that public schools with a large proportion of children of immigrants cease to belittle their ethnic heritage and values and devote a great part of their curricula to teaching the meaning and the process of production. Thus, she hoped, these future workers would understand the meaning of their work and see its worth and significance for themselves and for the society.

Children of the immigrants who were destined to go into specialized, often dull, jobs, would be helped if the schools would teach them where their jobs fit and how important they were in the total operation of the factory or the shop.

> If the shop constantly tends to make the working man a specialist, then the problem of the educator is clear: it is to give him what may be an offset from over-specialization of his daily work, to supply him with general information and to insist he shall be a cultivated member of society with a consciousness of his industrial and social value.

This may have been a naive approach because it assumed that the worker was interested in learning about the total operation of his factory and that that knowledge would help him to bear the hardships caused by low pay and bad working conditions. Combating the boredom of the workers on the assembly lines is still the preoccupation of many unions and employers today. In that area, too, Jane Addams was ahead of her time.

Her contemporaries have made Jane Addams, as Christopher Lasch observed, a saint and a national myth. The record seems to indicate that they were right on both counts.

5

Public Schools and the
Upward Mobility
of Immigrant Children

The great influx of immigrants from central, eastern, and southern Europe, which started about 1880, perplexed and often frightened professional and lay leaders of big-city public school systems in American large cities. There should be little surprise at this reaction. First, the size of the immigration was unprecedented. School boards and superintendents of school systems in New York, Chicago, Philadelphia, Boston, and other large cities were confronted with the task of educating many thousands of children of immigrants of all ages. These children knew no English. They spoke Italian, Yiddish, Polish, Russian, Czech, Serbian, or Croatian, had a variety of modes of behavior, and felt frightened and bewildered in their new American environment. Many of their parents, especially among the Italians, Poles, and Orthodox Jews had a suspicious and largely negative attitude to American schools, fearing that the school experience would alienate their children from them. Devoutly religious, they were apprehensive that their children would become prey to atheism and immorality or develop an antagonistic attitude to their native tongue and the values and mores of their group.

The complexity of the task of dealing with this great number of immigrant children ought not to be minimized. Some historians of education, and especially the leaders and the writers on "new ethnicity," have shown little understanding of the magnitude of this task. Michael Novak, Geno Baroni, and Barbara Mikulski who have written about the recent revival of ethnic awareness among several major ethnic groups are unsparing in criticizing the public schools for the effort to "Americanize" or to "melt" the children of the immigrants into the dominant Anglo-Saxon society. This seems to be a rather simplistic approach to the study of a complex social and educational problem.

Ethnic spokesmen assert that children of immigrants were forced by their insensitive, if not hostile, teachers to turn their backs on the cultural values of their parents. Consequently, they seem to be determined that the children of recently arrived immigrants do not suffer from the same disadvantage. Public school systems are asked to inaugurate bilingual and multi-cultural programs. Some spokesmen for Spanish-speaking minorities in large cities argue that it is not enough to give the children of Mexican and Puerto Rican parents instruction in Spanish in the transitional period until they are capable of making reasonable progress in English classes. They advocate a fully bilingual and bicultural education in Spanish and English not only for the Spanish immigrant children but for all the children attending school with them.

Bilingual Education Programs

Bilingual education as put into effect in Chicago, New York, Los Angeles, and Miami, is in essence bicultural education. Under these programs, students are to study the history, customs, and mores of Puerto Rico or Mexico or Cuba. The curriculum guide for bilingual education published by the Chicago Board of Education defines its objectives as follows:

> Bilingual education is a realistic approach to the educacational needs of thousands of boys and girls who must acquire positive self-concepts and communication skills in order to compete educationally, socially and economically as first-class citizens and full participants in today's society. For the child who comes from a non-English speaking background, bilingual education can also help maintain family loyalty. Programs that recognize a child's language and culture help to foster positive self-concepts in a youngster. Rather than becoming alienated from the cultural ties of his family, he will learn to enjoy and value diversity. The child who remains loyal to his family is more likely to develop allegiance to his family, to his school and country.

Those listed are benefits for Spanish-speaking children, but the authors of the guide advocate bilingualism for non-Spanish children who attend the same schools. They say:

> Non-English speaking children are not the only ones who stand to profit from bilingual education programs. English-speaking children who live in a community in which a second language is spoken will also have the opportunity to learn another language and become sensitive to another culture.

Some educators active in Spanish bilingual programs ask that the study of Spanish be made obligatory for white and black children attending school in Spanish-speaking neighborhoods, while others suggest that instruction in Spanish be voluntary.

The available evidence indicates that the leaders of the ethnic immigrant groups that came to the United States in large numbers around 1900 did not advocate bilingual or multi-cultural education. Even those who complained that public schools were alienating the young generation from their families wanted the schools to Americanize the immigrant children. Polish, Jewish, Italian, and Greek immigrant parents did not want the public schools to teach their children Polish, Yiddish, Italian, or Greek. Those who wanted their children to speak the language of their group sent them to Polish, Jewish, Italian, or Greek church or synagogue schools. One can argue that America may have not survived as a nation had these large immigrant groups, totaling many millions of people, succeeded in persuading the public schools to accept multi-lingual and multi-cultural education for all the children in the "Little Italies," and in the Jewish, Serbian, Polish, and Greek ghettos. Today bilingual education has considerable support in the Spanish-speaking communities in Chicago, New York, El Paso, Los Angeles, San Diego, and Miami and has been put in operation by many boards of education. Similar programs for bilingual education introduced in 1900 probably would have been rejected by the overwhelming majority of immigrants and would have met with unyielding resistance from the leaders of the public schools.

The reasons for the changed attitudes to multi-cultural education are complex but they can be sorted out. The United States of America was for millions of white immigrants a land of promise and opportunity, and to grasp this opportunity most of them were willing and even eager to pay the price of acculturation or assimilation to the dominant culture of their new society. Secondly, most of the immigrants looked upon the public school with awe and respect as the institution whose task it was to Americanize their children and give them the opportunity for social and economic advancement in the new country. The extent to which the public school succeeded in assuring the upward mobility of immigrant children is, of course, subject to different interpretations. But the immigrants' expectations for the schooling of their children explain why there was no demand for bilingual or multi-cultural education.

Many factors account for the acceptance by the leaders of the public school system today of the demands for bilingual and multi-cultural education. The prestige and the authority of the public school systems in New York,

Chicago, Los Angeles, and elsewhere are greatly diminished. Public school officials are on the defensive, under attack for meager scholastic accomplishments, and lack of order and discipline. A few school leaders find it difficult to resist the pressure exerted by the Spanish, black, and white ethnic groups, but most superintendents of schools in large cities and many school board members are convinced that the American society and its mainstream culture are so firmly rooted today, that bilingualism and multi-cultural education would not only not threaten but indeed may enrich the common American culture and strengthen the allegiance of the minority groups to the total American society.

The United States will not become a multi-ethnic and multi-cultural society. Those who make such demands are unrealistic and impractical. On the other hand, more modest programs for enriching the American cultural life, which finds itself under a severe challenge of changing values and conditions, by the study of cultural values and literary contributions of the cultures of the ethnic groups may well be an important contribution to the common good.

Ethnic Cultures and the Curriculum

The demand for the inclusion of materials on ethnicity and ethnic cultures in the school curriculum is usually coupled with attacks on the record of the public schools in educating the children of blacks and the immigrants. It is asserted that the public schools have failed to meet the expectations of the immigrants because they did not assure the upward social mobility of their children.

David Tyack excoriates the leaders of the public schools in the few decades before and after 1900 for the insensitive indoctrination of the children of the immigrants with Anglo-Saxon values. But the most sweeping indictment of the public schools was drawn up by Colin Greer in *The Great School Legend*. Historians of American education, says Greer, have long asserted that American public schools made a great contribution to the building of the American nation. The schools took "the backward poor, the ragged, ill-prepared ethnic minorities who crowded into the cities, educated and Americanized them into the homogeneous productive middle class that is America's strength and pride." This, according to Greer, is a false legend. The myth of the public school as an effective instrument for upward social mobility, as a ladder to economic progress and success for the poor, must be debunked, says Greer, if only to bring the present-day expectations of the blacks and Latinos for their children into line with reality. Many people assume that public schools today fail to provide effective education to the urban, black, and Latino poor while the schools in the past did just that for the white immigrant poor whom they lifted into the ranks of the middle class. Not so, says Greer. The record shows, he contends, that public schools did little or nothing for the children of the immigrants, and they cannot be expected to do much for the black, Spanish, and white poor children today.

To support this pessimistic view of the past and the present, Greer asserts that the children of the immigrants entered the public schools poor and uneducated and left them unprepared to take advantage of the opportunities presented by a rapidly growing industrial society. The evidence that Greer uses to support his revisionist view are school records of several big-city school systems. These records show, according to Greer, that the rate of failure and dropout among the urban poor, mostly children of the immigrants, before and since 1900, was remarkably high. "The truth is," Greer writes, "that the immigrant children dropped out in great numbers—to fall back on the customs and skills their families brought with them to America."

According to Greer, immigrant children were dropping out in great numbers because the schools failed to provide them with effective and meaningful education. This failure was not accidental. Public schools were in the past, and are now, the creatures and the servants of the American class structure. The public schools were created by the middle class to control, contain, and divert the lower classes; they exist to separate the successes and the failures along class lines. Public schools failed a great number of the children of the immigrants, Greer concludes, in order to feed them into the unskilled labor market.

Greer accuses historians of education of perpetuating the "great legend" because they blindly accepted the notion that the public school has a sacrosanct place in the "democratic rhetoric of the nation" and they have mistaken the "rhetoric of good intentions for historical reality." Among the misguided historians, Greer includes Oscar Handlin, Lawrence Cremin, and Henry Steele Commager. He quotes with disapproval a statement by Commager that "no other people ever demanded so much of its schools. . . . None was ever so well served by its schools and its educators. . . . To the schools went the momentous responsibility of . . . inculcating democracy, materialism and equalitarianism."

The data on the dropout rates in New York, Chicago, Philadelphia, Detroit, and Boston cited by Greer are taken from school surveys made by different people using different techniques and having different levels of competence. More importantly, the figures cited do not support Greer's conclusion that the schools were particularly unsuccessful with the immigrant children, because the statistics cited make no differentiation between native-born children and/or the children of immigrants, or between the children of the poor and those of middle- or upper-class parents.

It is of course true that many children of the immigrants dropped out from school at the age of 11 or 12. We have testimony to that effect in the writings of Jane Addams and in the records of the various settlement homes in New York, Boston, and other cities. Some dropped out because of poor teachers and irrelevant curricula but it is wrong for Greer to suggest that the sole responsibility for these dropouts was with the schools. Jane Addams has testified from firsthand experience that many parents of the immigrants connected with Hull House took their children, mostly boys, out of school at an early age so that they could supplement the family's income by working in shops or factories. Pressure for education or lack of it in the home of immigrants was often the decisive factor in whether or not a child stayed in school. Many Italian and Polish parents, for example, distrusted the public school not because of lack of scholastic effectiveness but because they feared that the school experience would alienate their children from their families, homes, and traditions. There was a particular concern that the girls would succumb to more relaxed sexual mores and bring shame to the families. The poverty with which the unskilled Italian immigrants had to cope often forced them to take the boys out of school because their earnings were needed to provide for the large families.

A detailed and carefully conducted survey of dropouts in the Chicago public schools and in the suburban schools in Cook County, Illinois, covering the 1973/74 school year, casts serious doubt on Greer's assumption that the rate of dropouts is a reliable measure of the success or the failure of schools. The Cook County school survey published in *The Chicago Tribune,* disclosed that of 145,878 students enrolled during the 1973/74 school year in the Chicago public schools, 21,456 dropped out. Out of 159,976 students attending schools in the Chicago suburbs, 5,279 were dropouts. An inquiry into the reasons for leaving school revealed that most of the dropouts, both in the city and in the suburbs, left for "no apparent reason," others left because "of lack of interest," some left because they wanted to work, a relatively few were expelled, and only a small proportion left because of uninteresting curricula or poor teaching. There is little reason to believe that the basic underlying reasons for the high rate of school dropouts in 1900 or 1910 or 1920 were different than they were in 1973. To base an indictment of public schools as having failed to provide the children of the immigrants with upward social mobility solely on the rate of dropouts does not seem to have much validity.

Immigrants and Public Education

To be sure the curriculum of the public schools at the turn of the century, at the height of the immigration waves, was often irrelevant to the interests and the needs of the students. John Dewey often charged that schools provided a poor preparation for success in life, but this was a general shortcoming from which all children and not only the children of the immigrants suffered. Many teachers were ineffective and poorly prepared, but this, too, was the result of the generally poor state of education and not a deliberate arrangement, as Greer would have us believe, on the part of the middle classes to provide inadequate education for the children of the immigrants and of the poor. Generally, schools were not prepared to deal with the unprecedented influx of many tens of thousands of immigrant children. The problem was indeed of staggering proportions. In 1909, according to a report published by the U.S. Commission of Immigration, 57.8 percent of the pupils attending schools in thirty-seven of the big cities were either foreign born or were children of immigrants. In New York the percentage was 71.5, and in Chicago 67.3.

If the United States were to survive and if the needs, the demands, and the hopes of the immigrants for their children were to be met, and at least partially fulfilled, public schools had to perform the difficult task of assimilating or acculturating and adjusting these children to the American environment, the American culture, and to the new society. The problem was complicated by the authoritarian and inflexible character of most public schools at the turn of the century. The following description of a public school in New York in 1893, written by Joseph Rice who visited schools in thirty-six cities, undoubtedly fits many other schools in big population centers:

> The typical New York City primary school is a hard unsympathetic, mechanized drudgery school, a school into which the light of science has not yet entered. Its characteristic feature is in the severity of its discipline, a discipline of enforced silence, immobility and mental passivity.

> The primary reading is, as a rule so poor that the children
> are scarcely able to recognize new words at sight at the
> end of the second year. Even the third year reading is
> miserable.

As we shall see there were schools in New York City where
the picture was brighter.

Some teachers, by no means all, had little sympathy
for the alien immigrant children and were impatient to
have them shed their "foreignness" as soon as possible.
Oscar Handlin says in *The Uprooted* of such a teacher,
"Casually she could twist the knife of ridicule in the sore-
ness of their sensibilities; there was so much in their accents, appearance and manners that were open to
mockery!" On the other hand, as we shall see, many
teachers helped and encouraged able immigrant children
far beyond the call of duty.

Many thousands of immigrant children, Jewish, Polish,
Greek, Italian, Slovak, whose parents encouraged them to
learn did well in the public schools. They learned English
and went through the elementary schools into colleges and
became successful doctors, lawyers, engineers, and businessmen. Mary Antin, who came to this country from
Russia as a child with her immigrant parents, wrote of her
teachers in the public school in Chelsea, Massachusetts,
with gratitude and affection. They encouraged her to become a writer and her book of reminiscences, *The Promised
Land,* became a best-seller and went through thirty-four
printings. About her entrance into the public school Antin
wrote:

> The apex of my civic pride and personal contentment
> was reached on the bright September morning when I en-
> tered public school. The day I must always remember,
> even if I live to be so old that I cannot tell my name . . .
> for I was led to the school room, with its sunshine and the
> teacher's cheery smile. . . .

To Mary Antin and to many immigrant children as well
as to many of the older immigrants, America was a liberat-
ing experience, truly a land of promise and opportunity.

"Father himself," Antin wrote, "conducted us to the

school. He would not have delegated that mission to the President of the United States. He had awaited the day with impatience equal to mine, and the visions he saw as he hurried us over the sun-flecked pavements transcended all my dreams. Almost his first act on landing on American soil, three years before, had been his application for naturalization. He had taken the remaining steps in the process with eager promptness, and the earliest moment allowed by law he became a citizen of the United States." "The public school," Mary Antin concluded, "has done its best for us foreigners and for the country when it made us into good Americans."

A. R. Dugmore, a writer of some renown, visited in 1903 a public school in New York, where almost all students were children of immigrants and liked what he saw.

> The pupils are of different nationalities or races that have their separate quarters in the immediate neighborhood. The majority of the pupils are Swedes, Austrians, Greeks, Russians, English, Irish, Scotch, Welsh, Rumanians, Italians, Poles, Hungarians, Canadians, Armenians, Germans, Chinese, and a very large number of Jews.
>
> The most noticeable thing in the school is the perfectly friendly equality in which all these races mix; no prejudice is noticeable. . . . It is a large task that schools of this kind are doing, taking the new, low-class foreign boys of many nationalities and molding them into self-supporting and self-respecting citizens of the republic . . . these boys and girls of foreign parentage readily catch the simple ideas of American ideas of independence and individual work and with them, social progress.

To Michael Novak on the other hand, the story of the immigrants and of their experiences in American schools is an unmitigated tale of woe, suffering, and discrimination. He wrote recently in an article published in *The Center Magazine:* "One of the greatest and most dramatic migrations of human history brought more than thirty million immigrants to this land between 1874 and 1924. Despite the immense dramatic materials involved in this migration, only one major American film records it: Elia

Kazan's *America! America!* That film ends with the arrival of the hero in America. The tragic and costly experience of Americanization has scarcely yet been touched. How many died; how many were morally and psychologically destroyed; how many still carry the marks of changing their names, of 'killing' their mother tongue and renouncing their former identity, in order to become 'new men' and 'new women,' there are motifs of violence, self-mutilation, joy, and irony. The inner history of this migration must come to be understood if we are ever to understand the aspirations and fears of some seventy million Americans."

Was Americanization a joyous experience as Mary Antin saw it or was it a tragedy as Michael Novak evaluates it now? Whose story are we to believe? It would seem that both views have some truth in them. No generalization about an immigration of 30 or 40 million people could withstand a rigorous testing because the evidence is contradictory. For many immigrants the Antin experience was true but for others Novak's account conformed to reality. The experiences of several of the immigrant groups differed in accordance with their background and aspirations. What was true for the Greeks was not necessarily true for the Serbs and the Croats. There were some Jews who did not look upon America as the promised land and not all of them became socially and economically successful and not *all* Slovaks, Poles, and Italians resented the melting process into the American cultural patterns. Some welcomed it and used it as an opportunity for advancement and many of them are grateful to America for absorbing and assimilating them.

We have said that public schools were generally of poor quality, with low standards and antiquated curricula but it must also be noted that the influx of immigrant children brought important reforms which greatly facilitated their education and the adjustment of their parents to the new environment. Elwood Cubberley, had, as we have seen, little sympathy for the immigrants but he advocated and supported special programs to teach immigrant children

English more effectively. He used his great influence for the establishment of evening schools for those immigrant adolescents who worked during the day. He stated, in *Public Education in the United States,* "Evening elementary schools are chiefly useful, in states enforcing a good compulsory education law in providing the foreign born with the elements of English education and in preparing would be voters for citizenship."

Cubberley also came out for transforming the public schools into community centers serving adults, in their own neighborhoods, with a variety of courses. "We see now," he wrote, "that our schools must at once take on another new function, that of providing special classes and night schools, on an adequate scale that will induct the foreign born into the use of English as his common speech, and prepare him for naturalization by training him in the history and principles of our government." In hundreds of cities according to the records of the U.S. Bureau of Education, school houses were made to function as community centers in the evenings and hundreds of thousands of immigrants took courses in English, American History, and civics.

School systems in large cities, including New York City, Chicago, Boston, and many others introduced reforms and educational innovations which greatly benefitted the immigrant children. Some of these reforms came as a consequence of the general mood for reforms in the Progressive Era, others were directly related to the efforts by lay and professional school leaders to make the education of immigrant children more effective. Critics of the public schools and some of the revisionist historians of education tend to dismiss these reforms and improvements as part of the crass or ruthless scheme to "Americanize" the children of the immigrants and to force upon them the mores and values of the dominant society. This judgment seems to be superficial and unfair. Of course, Americanization was a cherished objective but the tremendous and many-faceted progress made by the public school systems in large cities in the period between 1890 and 1920 was beneficial to immigrant and native children alike and to the general society, as well. Furthermore, many reforms had nothing to do with the Americanization efforts. They were related largely to a more progressive and more humane conception of the role of education and of schooling in an industrial and democratic society and resulted from a genuine concern for making schooling more effective for the many thousands of immigrant children.

In New York City, many school reforms were initiated by William H. Maxwell who became Superintendent of Schools in 1898. Maxwell's interest in the education of immigrant children may have stemmed, at least in part, from the discrimination he himself suffered after his arrival in the United States from Northern Ireland where he was a teacher. Because he was a foreigner, he could not get a job for many years. After working for several years as a newspaper man, he finally got a teaching position in Brooklyn. Maxwell built many new schools, especially in areas of great concentration of immigrants, including the Lower East Side and the "Little Italy" around Mulberry Street. Most of the new schools were equipped with spacious playgrounds, libraries, and gymnasia. They served in the evenings as adult centers for adults. The school curriculum was greatly expanded to include instruction in physical education, science, health and hygiene, sewing, and even in etiquette and manners. Since 1909, Maxwell added a string of vocational schools which taught immigrants and native children carpentry, plumbing, and other artisan skills.

Taking note of the poverty in many immigrant slum areas of the city, the Board of Education instituted free breakfast and lunch programs. To make the food more palatable special ethnic foods, like Jewish kosher meals and Italian pasta dishes were served in the city's Jewish and Italian areas.

Absenteeism and the dropout rate were very high in schools where immigrant children abounded. It is indicative of the genuine concern for the education of the immigrants that since 1903, several laws were promulgated to extend the compulsory attendance age limit and to combat truancy. Most significantly, special, so called "C" classes, were organized to provide intensive instruction in English to older immigrant children in order to enable them to enter regular classes in the shortest time.

What happened in New York was largely duplicated in Chicago, Philadelphia, Boston, and in smaller cities with large concentrations of immigrants. In Gary, Indiana, where Croats, Poles, Serbs, Bohemians, and Jews settled in large numbers because of the concentration of steel mills, the public schools were headed by William Wirt, one of the most authoritarian, imaginative, innovative, and controversial educators in America. Wirt made no bones about his objective of molding the children of the immigrants into patriotic, virtuous, and hard-working Americans. To accomplish this objective, he built in Gary many school buildings which were the showplaces of school architecture in the nation. Gary schools had splendid gymnasia with large swimming pools and large auditoria equipped with theatre stages and fine libraries. Regular public schools and the many vocational schools that were built under Wirt's leadership were open in the evenings and thousands of children and parents used the sport facilities and took advantage of adult classes and lectures. In order to provide a closer link between school and home, teachers were required to make regular visits to the homes of their pupils.

Wirt introduced a twelve-month school program on a platoon basis. Students were in the schoolrooms only half a day and spent the rest of the day in vocational shops and other work centers. The "Gary Plan" was widely imitated throughout the country.

Wirt was an outspoken advocate of a rapid process of Americanization of the immigrant children. He had little regard for the ethnic cultures of the immigrants. However, there is no record of a significant opposition to Wirt on the issue of Americanization. On the contrary, Wirt seemed to have enjoyed a great measure of support from the parents, the press, the clergy, and from the Gary community at large, throughout his long tenure. Apparently, the multi-ethnic city of Gary believed that their public schools were good for their children.

Mary Antin's happy experience in the public schools was not unique. Another equally popular autobiography of an immigrant attests that some immigrants from eastern Europe looked with favor on their melting experience. In 1923, the famous inventor and professor of electro-mechanics at Columbia University, Michael Pupin, published his memoirs under the title, *From Immigrant to Inventor*. The book was widely acclaimed and went through twenty-five editions. It was bought and read until the late 1940s. Pupin immigrated to America from a Serb village in 1874, at the age of nineteen. In a chapter entitled "The Hardships of a Green Horn," Pupin describes the hardships he suffered in working on farms and factories in Delaware and New Jersey and New York, but he also relates the many kindnesses he received from total strangers. When he enrolled at Columbia College, while still a factory worker, his professors were kind, understanding, and very encouraging. He was soon elected class president. "But when American college boys . . . elected for class president" he wrote, "the penniless son of a Serbian peasant village, because they admire his mental and physical efforts to learn and to comply with Columbia's traditions, one can rest assured that the spirit of American democracy was very much alive in those college boys." Pupin "made it" and became a distinguished professor at Columbia. He, as he points out in his memoirs, retained his pride in the Serbian culture, language, and the Serbian Orthodox Church, while enthusiastically cherishing his American citizenship. Michael Novak has testified that his "making it" as a university professor was a painful experience for him because he felt compelled to give up the ties to his Slovak family and community. These contradictory accounts only affirm the fact that it is impossible and unwise to generalize about experiences of millions of immigrants who came to the United States from many countries and many different cultural religious backgrounds.

Admittedly, American education was, at the turn of the 20th century, almost exclusively dominated by men and women who believed that one of the important tasks of the public schools was to help the children of immigrants to assimilate, as quickly and as painlessly as possible, into the common American culture.

Cubberley defined his objective in *Public Education in the United States:*

> Our task is to assimilate or amalgamate these people as part of the American race, and to implant in their children, so far as can be done, the Anglo-Saxon conception of righteousness, law, order, and popular government, and to awaken in them reverence for our democratic institutions and for those things which we as people hold to be of abiding worth.

Commenting on this quote from Cubberley, Professor Rudolph Vecoli of the University of Minnesota (in his testimony before the Pucinski Subcommittee) said: "It is clear that Cubberley wished not to Americanize, but to Anglo-Saxonize the little immigrants." Granted that the tone of superiority and the plea for indoctrination grates on our ears, one ought to ask whether the *objectives* as defined by Cubberley were faulty. Was it not necessary to teach the thousands of children of Poles, Italians, Serbs, Croatians, and Jews, whose parents, for good reasons, considered the law, the police, and all government officials in their countries of origin as tools of oppression and persecution, that law, police, and governmental authority were different in America? And was it not necessary to give them some understanding of the nature and the operation of the American democratic institutions?

The "Mainstream" American Culture

And finally, was it desirable or even essential that the immigrants and especially their children understand the cultural values and mores of the mainstream American culture? This question poses a problem that must be discussed at some length. What was the mainstream American

culture around the year 1900? Present-day spokesmen for
the white ethnic group refer rather contemptuously to that
culture as WASP or Anglo-Saxon. But is it indeed true
that the immigrants who came to New York, Chicago,
Boston, and Los Angeles at the turn of the century encountered the Puritan Calvinistic ethic and culture that
make Novak so unhappy?

There are few studies of American culture and American national character. The best research in that area was
done by the late Berkeley historian, David Potter. In his
book, *People of Plenty: Economic Abundance and the
American Character,* published in 1954, Potter suggested
that relative economic prosperity accounts for American
traits like mobility, aggressiveness, and an affinity for
competition. In a later essay, Potter asserted that both the
American culture and American character are rooted in
the immigrant origin of the American people. The only
people in America who are true Americans, Potter affirmed, are the Indians; all other Americans are immigrants. Americans, in time, became united by important
characteristics and common values. Without these common
commitments and common respect for certain qualities of
character, customs, and values, there could never have
been an American nationality.

> It is partly for this reason that Americans, although com-
> mitted to the principle of freedom of thought, have never-
> theless placed such a heavy emphasis upon the obligation
> to accept certain undefined tenets of "Americanism."

This profound observation may help explain the fear that
gripped many native Americans when confronted with
huge immigration waves of millions of foreigners. They
simply were not sure that America was yet a united nation, bound by common values and able to withstand the
influence of masses of people with different cultural values
and mores. Thus, what appeared to the immigrants as
Anglo-Saxon arrogance and a sense of superiority may
have been in fact the manifestations of a feeling of insecurity by a nation still in its formative state.

The antipathy and the ridicule that confronted some of

the immigrants in the United States ought to be put in perspective by a comparison with the contemporary attitude of native populations in other countries toward aliens in their midst. In the last few decades, we have seen the law-abiding people of Great Britain in a veritable turmoil over the immigration of a few hundred thousand West Indians and Pakistanis. Powerful voices warned that continued immigration would undermine the English society and subvert its values and institutions. Public opinion finally forced the British government to severely limit immigration. The law passed in Parliament had the overwhelming support of both major parties, the Conservatives and the Socialist Labor Party.

The 800,000 Algerians in France, most of whom came there after World War II, have yet to be accepted by the French people. They are harassed, ridiculed, and persecuted by the police and by large segments of the population. The several hundred thousands of Yugoslavs, Italians, and Turks who are imported to West Germany as temporary workers for jobs the Germans do not wish to do, are held in open contempt by the German population. In many German cities, the immigrants are often jeered at and even beaten by hostile mobs. German political leaders vie with each other in declaring that the ingress of immigrants must stop. Immigrant laborers in civilized Holland and Belgium find themselves in a similar predicament. No government in the European Common Market countries would dare to allow many of these foreigners to become permanent residents. Contrasted with this situation in the enlightened 1970s, the record of America on the immigration issue looks quite good.

What culture confronted the immigrants on the American soil? Observers of the American scene, both foreign and native, who travelled extensively in the United States never perceived the American mainstream culture as it appears to Novak or Greeley. They did not see it as an Anglo-Saxon or British-American culture. On the contrary, they all saw in it *uniquely* American features closely tied to the American experience in a new, vast country. Alexis de Tocqueville, the brilliant French aristocrat, observed in 1836 that for the Americans "Liberty is not the chief object of their desires, equality is their idol. They make rapid and sudden efforts to obtain liberty, . . . but nothing can satisfy them without equality, and they would rather perish than lose it." English writers Harriett Martineau and Charles Dickens, who traveled extensively in the United States, found little Anglo-Saxon or British in the character or the behavior of the Americans. In fact, Dickens heartily disliked almost everything he saw in America, especially its crude, impatient, and aggressive people, bent on preaching and practicing equalitarianism.

Frederick Jackson Turner concluded in his famous 1893 essay, "The Significance of the Frontier in American History," that America's national character and culture owed much less to the English heritage than to the conditions of living on the frontier. According to Turner, life on the frontier, which gradually shifted from the Eastern Seaboard to the Far West, forced Americans to be self-reliant, inventive, practical, aggressive, and mobile individualists. There was no other way for them to carve out a civilization from a wilderness in a hostile environment. Turner declared,

> The American intellect owes its striking characteristics to the frontier. That coarseness and strength, combined with acuteness and acquisitiveness; that practical turn of mind, quick to find expedients . . . that restless nervous energy; that dominant individualism . . . these are traits of the frontier, or traits called out elsewhere because of the existence of the frontier.

Americans were individualists, as Turner saw them, but they were also conformists, as de Tocqueville observed. In modern terms, used by David Riesman in *The Lonely Crowd*, Americans are either "inner-directed" or "other-directed." Using the frontier experience as a frame of reference, there is no contradiction between these two characteristics. Americans in the seventeenth and eighteenth centuries were mostly self-employed, living in relative physical isolation, but they needed the help of their neighbors in the face of natural disaster or hostile Indians. No wonder, then, that Americans are today both individualists and enthusiastic joiners of clubs and organizations.

The discussion of the native American culture and of the American national character, as it was already formed by the time of the Great Migration, is pertinent to a consideration of the relationship between the native American society and the immigrants and to the role of the schools in educating the children of the immigrants. It would seem that the mainstream culture that confronted the immigrants was not the Puritan, Anglo-Saxon culture but an *already melted American culture*. The immigrants found an American nation that exhibited and cherished character traits and values forged by the frontier experience on the American soil. As Daniel Boorstin has shown in his works on American social history, American political institutions, the schools, and the courts were mainly the product of American experience, not imported from England or from Europe, but pragmatically formed to answer the needs of Americans in their new land. No wonder, then, that many immigrants found this new American culture so attractive and were eager to imitate and internalize the commonly cherished traits of the American character.

In this light, the special love shown by the immigrants for American history and their worship of Washington and Lincoln become readily understandable. The present-day writers on ethnicity and the immigrant experience do violence to historical truth when they write about coercive efforts to mold the immigrants to conform to an *Anglo-Saxon* culture, which in fact the immigrants did not confront because it did not exist.

To be sure, the process of assimilating the immigrants and their children to the American culture was often crude and insensitive. Members of the American education establishment and the school superintendents in the big cities, most of them of English stock, perceived it to be their duty to make the public schools the most efficient instruments for transmission of American culture to native and immigrant children alike. All were to be taught to accept the American system of values and ideas. Education for living in the American democratic society was the goal of schooling, with the clear implication that that society was far superior to the mode of living so dear to the hearts of most immigrant parents. Most educators and teachers profoundly believed in the sacred mission of Americanization and had an abiding faith in the ability of the American environment and of American education to transform human nature. The "refuse of Europe" was to be bettered and ennobled by the infusion of American values and ideas.

Granting that the "Americanization" of hundreds of thousands of children of immigrants was often a painful experience, the fact is that it was eminently successful. Even more important, it was necessary if a "nation of immigrants" was to remain a nation with a common culture. Public schools were the basic workshop of American democracy where ethnic and religious differences were de-emphasized, where children of many races began to look upon themselves as Americans, and where they learned to live together and to take advantage of the opportunities of American freedom. Handlin, in *Immigration as a Factor in American History,* chastises some of the teachers for ignoring ethnic sensibilities, but he emphasizes the role of the schools in providing the opportunity for upward mobility for the immigrants. However, Peter Schrag, in *The Decline of the WASP,* complains that the immigrants had to pay a price for their advancement. "If you wanted to advance," he says, "you paid a price, changed your name, junked your accent, named your children Lynn and Shelley, and you didn't mind their growing contempt for your ethnicity." All this is true, but millions of ethnics did not mind paying the price of admission to American society. Many paid it with joy and gratitude.

Jewish grandparents and parents had an abiding love for the public schools because they opened new opportunities for their children. The American public school, in which there were no compulsory religious prayers and where Jewish children were not an isolated and despised minority, was incomparably better than the schools in Poland, Russia, Serbia, Hungary, or Slovenia. The shortening of long, unpronounceable names, which were originally imposed on Jewish families by hostile Russian county clerks, and the substitution of English for Yiddish, was, in most cases readily accepted.

Most Jewish parents welcomed every outward evidence that their children were becoming Americanized. A child who asked for a baseball, a bat, and a glove brought smiles of pride and tears of joy to the eyes of his parents. It was a sign that he was becoming a "real" American. Surely, the rapid assimilation of the young, their abandonment of religious practices, the unwillingness to attend Yiddish or Hebrew afternoon schools, was painful to some parents, especially those who were orthodox. On balance, however, most Jews *wanted* to pay the price of admission to the dominant society. They thought the price to be a reasonable one for the opportunity to live in a country where freedom and equality, while not universally practiced, were deeply ingrained constitutional principles.

The same was undoubtedly true of millions of Germans and Scandinavians and, with some exceptions, of millions of Poles, Italians, Irish, and other immigrants who escaped from foreign or domestic oppression and from abject conditions of poverty. For the children of immigrants, the education they received in the public schools represented the gate to opportunity. The public schools and the universities fulfilled their assigned roles more than adequately. Those ethnic leaders who today deride the record of the public schools ought to remember that their parents and grandparents valued the public schools as one of the most important American institutions and demanded, often by the use of corporal punishment, obedience and respect for the teachers.

A balanced assessment of the record of the public schools will also have to include the recognition of the fact that it was precisely one of the values in the WASP

ethic that affirmed the freedom of the immigrant groups
to practice their faith and to adhere to their values. This
basic principle in the American Creed made the preservation of ethnic differences possible. To suggest, as Professor
Vecoli did, that Americanization was similar to the ruthless
attempt to Germanize the Poles, an attempt bolstered by
laws and governmental regulations, is a distortion of the
record of history. According to Oscar Handlin,

> Americanization did not make all groups alike or destroy
> their ethnic quality. Not only did traditions retain their
> strength but the very conditions of co-existence in a plural-
> istic society created the assumption that each man would
> adhere to the faith of his fathers.

Many groups in the American society were unwilling to
pay the price and did not want to "make it" on WASP
terms, but they suffered no great misfortune, and still
thrive. One million Cajuns in Louisiana still speak some
French and adhere to their own cultural mores, and yet
they can boast of their growing economic and political
power. In 1971, a French-speaking Cajun was elected
governor of the state. The same is true of the Chinese-
Americans, the Amish, the Hassidim in Brooklyn, and
others. Of course, these groups preserved their separate
identity by imposing upon themselves a large degree of
isolation from the general society. This is a price that
many other immigrant groups were unwilling to pay.

On the whole, however, the process of assimilation of the
large ethnic groups, the Irish, the Poles, the Jews, and the
Italians, has been quite successful. In spite of what the
ethnic leaders tell us, the melting pot is neither a dead
myth nor a failure. In fact, that theory worked remarkably
well, on the whole. It is estimated that the United States
between the years 1880 and 1920, absorbed about 40 million immigrants, mainly from Ireland, Scandinavia, Germany, and central and southern Europe. Millions of children and grandchildren of these former Irishmen, Germans,
Swedes, Poles, Italians, and others have indeed "melted."
They consider themselves, and are considered by others,
as "just Americans." Some of them cut the ties to their

ethnic groups in order to advance economically and socially in the dominant society, but many were attracted by
the rich American culture and heritage and felt no need to
cherish old memories and loyalties. The descendants of
Americans who came to the United States from colonial
times and onward, and the descendants of the hundreds
and thousands of pioneers who settled the Western frontier
areas have also, with some exceptions, shed any ties they
had with their respective ethnic communities. The heroes
of the conquest of the West, Daniel Boone, David Bridger,
Wyatt Earp, Judge Bean, Matt Dillon were Americans who
forgot or disregarded their ethnic origins. Accurate figures
on white ethnic communities in the United States are hard
to come by, but even if we accept the exaggerated figure
of 40 million white ethnics, and add to it 20 million blacks
and 10 million Spanish-Americans, that still leaves over
150 million people in America who have no particular
ethnic affiliation.

In addition, there is an infinite variety of modes of
identification of those who do have some ethnic loyalties.
An ethnic identification scale may start with a young mar-
ried couple whose parents were born in Germany and who
do not speak German, belong to no German-American organization but like "sauerbraten," to Meir Kahane of the
Jewish Defense League, who has despaired of the American
society and urges a mass exodus of Jews from the United
States to Israel. The varieties of ethnic identification between those two extremes cannot even be catalogued.

Jews in America are *American* Jews; Italians are
American Italians; and Poles are *American* Poles. The
same is true of other white ethnic groups. The "American"
component is not easy to define, but ethnically conscious
Americans seem to be quite clear about their Americanism. They often make the point that loyalty to their ethnic
group made them better and prouder Americans.

The public schools, the evening schools, and the settlement houses played an important role in the absorption
of the millions of immigrants. Gunnar Myrdal, the Swedish
sociologist, has devoted many years to the study of the

American society. In a recent article in *The Center Magazine,* he made this sound observation on the role of the public schools in the period of large-scale immigration:

> Throughout this long period, the immigrants came almost entirely from the lower social and economic strata in their home countries. All had to start from the bottom and work themselves up, a process aided by the public school system, which, with all its defects, was a relatively efficient vehicle for social mobility, even it if took a generation or two to climb the ladder.

SELECTED BIBLIOGRAPHY

Addams, Jane. *Twenty Years of Hull House*. New York: Macmillan Co., 1938.

_____. *Democracy and Social Ethics*. Cambridge, Mass.: Harvard University Press, 1902.

_____. *The Second Twenty Years at Hull House*. New York: The Macmillan Company, 1930.

The American Jewish Committee. *Group Life in America, A Task Force Report*. New York: The American Jewish Committee, 1972.

Antin, Mary. *The Promised Land*. Boston: Houghton Mifflin Co., 1911.

Bailey, Harry A., Jr., and Katz, Ellis (eds.). *Ethnic Group Politics*. Columbus, Ohio: Charles Merrill Co., 1969.

Baroni, G. "Ethnicity and Public Policy," in M. Henk, S. M. Tomasi, and G. Baroni, (eds.). *Pieces of a Dream*. New York: Center for Migration Studies, 1972.

Blalock, H. M., Jr. *Toward a Theory of Minority-Group Relations*. New York: Wiley, 1967.

Cahan, Abraham. *The Rise of David Levinsky*. New York: Harper and Row Publishing, 1960.

Chandler, B. J., Stiles, Lindley, and Kitsuse, John I. *Education in Urban Society*. Dodd, Mead, 1962.

Chicago Board of Education. *A Comprehensive Design for Bilingual Education*. 2d ed. Chicago: Board of Education, 1973.

Cook, Ann, Grittell, Marilyn, and Mack, Herb (eds.). *City Life, 1865-1900: Views of Urban America*. New York: Praeger Publishers, 1973.

Cubberley, Elwood P. *Changing Conceptions of Education*. New York: Riverside Educational Mimeographs, 1909.

_____. *Public Education in the United States*. Boston: Houghton Mifflin Co., 1919.

Davis, Allen F. *American Heroine—The Life and Legend of Jane Addams*. New York: Oxford University Press, 1973.

De Tocqueville, Alexis. *Democracy in America*. New York: Alfred A. Knopf, 1946.

Ethnic Heritage Centers. *Hearings before the General Sub-Committee on Education of the Committee on Education and Labor, House of Representatives.* Washington, D.C.: Government Printing Office, 1970.

Fairchild, Henry Pratt. *The Melting Pot Mistake.* Boston: Little, Brown & Co., 1926.

Franklin, John Hope, Pettigrew, Thomas F., Mark, Raymond W. *Ethnicity in American Life.* New York: Anti-Defamation League of B'nai B'rith, 1971.

Fuchs, Lawrence H. (ed.). *American Ethnic Politics.* New York: Harper and Row, 1968.

Glazer, Nathan and Moynihan, Patrick. *Beyond the Melting Pot.* Cambridge, Mass.: M.I.T. Press, 1963.

Gordon, Milton. *Assimilation in American Life.* New York: Oxford Press, 1964.

Greeley, Andrew M. *Why Can't They Be Like Us?* New York: American Jewish Committee Institute of Human Relations Press, 1969.

Greer, Colin. *The Great School Legend: A Revisionist Interpretation of American Education.* New York: Basic Books, 1972.

Handlin, Oscar. *Immigration as a Factor in American History.* Englewood Cliffs, N.J.: Prentice-Hall, 1959.

Hansen, Marcus Lee. *The Immigrant in American History.* New York: Harper Torch Books, 1940.

Hawkins, W. Brett and Lorinkas, A. Robert, (eds.). *The Ethnic Factor in American Politics.* Columbus, Ohio: Charles Merrill Publishing Co., 1970.

——————. *The Uprooted.* Boston: Little Brown and Company, 1952.

Hertz, Alexander. *Reflections on America (Refleksje Amerikanskie).* Paris: Institute Literacki, 1966.

Higham, John. *Strangers in the Land.* New York: Atheneum, 1968.

Howe, Irwing (ed.). *The World of Blue Collar Workers.* New York: Quadrangle Books, 1972.

Iorizzo, J. Luciano, and Mondello, Salvatore. *The Italian-Americans.* New York: Twayne Publishing Co., 1971.

Karier, Clarence J., Violas, Paul, and Spring, Joel. *Roots of Crisis*. Chicago: Rand McNally, 1973.

Kallen, Horace M. *Cultural Pluralism and the American Idea*. Philadelphia: University of Philadelphia Press, 1956.

Kusielewicz, Eugene. *Reflections on the Cultural Conditions of the Polish-American Community*. New York: Czas Publishing Co., 1969.

Lasch, Christopher (ed.). *The Social Thought of Jane Addams*. Indianapolis: Bobbs Merrill Co., 1965.

_____. *The New Radicalism in America, 1889-1963*. New York: Vintage Books, 1967.

Litt, Edgar. *Ethnic Politics in America*. Glenview, Ill.: Scott Foresman, Co., 1970.

Mann, Arthur. *Immigrants in American Life: Selected Readings*. New York: Houghton Mifflin, 1973.

Nelli, Humbert S. *Italians in Chicago*. New York: Oxford University Press, 1970.

Novak, Michael. *The Rise of the Unmeltable Ethnics*. New York: Macmillan Co., 1971.

Parson, Talcott. *Structure and Process in Modern Societies*. Glencoe, Ill.: The Free Press, 1960.

Pettigrew, T. F. *Racially Separate or Together?* New York: McGraw-Hill, 1971.

Pupin, Michael. *From Immigrant to Inventor*. New York: Charles Scribner's Sons, 1926.

Polish American Congress, Inc. *Polonia in the Seventies: New Challenges*. Chicago: Polish American Congress, 1972.

Potter, David M. *History and American Society*. New York: Oxford University Press, 1973.

Puzo, Mario. *The Fortunate Pilgrim*. New York: Lancer Books, 1964.

Rischin, Moses. *The Promised City*. New York: Harper, Torch Books, 1962.

Schrag, Peter. *The Decline of the WASP*. New York: Simon and Schuster, 1971.

Shannon, William V. *The American Irish*. New York: Macmillan, 1967.

Thomas, William and Znaniecki, Florian. *The Polish Peasant in Europe and in America.* New York: Dove Publication, 1958.

Tomasi, Silvano M., and Engel, Madeline H. (eds.). *The Italian Experience in the United States.* Staten Island, N.Y.: Center for Migration Studies, 1970.

Turner, Frederick J. *The Frontier in American History.* New York: Henry Holt Co., 1920.

Warner, W. Lloyd, and Srole, Leo. *The Social Systems of American Ethnic Groups.* (Yankee City Studies.) New Haven: Yale University Press, 1945.

Wirth, Louis. *The Ghetto.* Chicago: University of Chicago Press, 1928.

_____ . *On Cities And Social Life.* Chicago: University of Chicago Press, 1964.

Wyrtwal, Joseph A. *Poles in American History and Tradition.* Detroit: Michigan Endurance Press, 1962.

Zangwill, Israel. *The Melting Pot.* New York: Macmillan Co., 1910.

Index

shops—70-71; unions—42, 59
Lasch, Christopher—66, 68, 77
Lincoln, Abraham—10, 17, 99
Lipset, Seymour Martin—59
literacy—24, 28-29, 36, 38, 40-41
literature, ethnic—17-18, 36, 51-52
Lithuania—24, 28, 30
Lithuanian-Americans—4, 60-61
Lithuanian Catholic Church—21
"Little Italies"—25-28, 53, 82, 92
Loneley Crowd, The—98
Lord's Prayer—21
Louisiana—4, 102

"Macaroni Hills"—25
Mafia—28, 52, 55
Magyars—7
Mahan, Alfred—18
Mailer, Norman—19
Malamud, Bernard—19
Martineau, Harriett—98
Maryland
    Baltimore—50
    Baltimore City Council—4
Massachusetts
    Boston—56, 58, 79, 85, 91, 93, 96
    Chelsea—88
Maxwell, William H.—92
May, Henry—18
Mazewski, Aloysius—42
Mazzini, Giuseppi—71
McCarthy, Mary—19
Melting Pot, The—10
Melting Pot Mistake, The—12
melting pot theory—vs. "Americanization"—viii, 6-10, 12-14;
    immigrant ethnic awareness—4-5; 15; history of—10-12;
    Jane Addams—74; public education—80, 94, 102
Mexican-Americans—80
Michigan
    Detroit—38, 43, 85
    Orchard Lake—19, 51
Mickiewicz, Adam—35, 36